# WHAT'SINSTYLE
# OUTDOOR
# LIVING

# WHAT'S IN STYLE
# OUTDOOR LIVING

Karin Strom

CREATIVE HOMEOWNER®, Upper Saddle River, New Jersey

**CRE🏠TIVE**
HOMEOWNER®

A Division of Federal Marketing Corp.
Upper Saddle River, NJ

**Editorial Director:** Timothy O. Bakke
**Production Manager:** Kimberly H. Vivas

**Senior Editor, Home Decorating:** Kathie Robitz
**Editor, Home Decorating:** Therese Hoehlein Cerbie
**Photo Editor:** Stanley Sudol
**Copy Editor:** Ellie Sweeney
**Editorial Assistants:** Dan Houghtaling, Sharon Ranftle
**Indexer:** Schroeder Indexing Services

**Book Designer:** Stephanie Phelan
**Graphic Designer:** Scott Molenaro
**Cover Design:** Glee Barre
**Front Cover Photography:** Tim Street-Porter, Beate Works
**Back Cover Photography:** (upper right) John Glover; (left) Ken Druse; (lower right) Tria Giovan

**Designer Tips:** Diane Boyer, ASID, Diane Boyer Interiors, a div. of Bill Behrle Associates, Verona, NJ; Judith Driscoll, Judith Driscoll Interior Design, St. Paul, MN; Janet Lohman, Janet Lohman Interior Design, Los Angeles, CA; Lyn Peterson, Motif Designs, New Rochelle, NY; Miranda Smith, Horticulturist, South Hadley, MA; Marlene Wangenheim, ASID, Interiors By Design, Bernardsville, NJ.

Manufactured in the United States of America

Current Printing (last digit)
10 9 8 7 6 5 4 3 2 1

What's in Style—Outdoor Living
Library of Congress Control Number: 2001090771
ISBN: 1-58011-114-9

CREATIVE HOMEOWNER®
A Division of Federal Marketing Corp.
24 Park Way, Upper Saddle River, NJ 07458
Web site: **www.creativehomeowner.com**

# acknowledgments

*When I began this project in the dead of winter, it was the beautiful photographs that inspired me to believe that another season of outdoor living would indeed arrive . . . eventually. Thanks to all who helped me to complete it in time to return to my own backyard oasis—especially Kathie Robitz and Terry Cerbie.*

# contents

# introduction

You can enjoy **stylish,** versatile, and relaxed indoor/outdoor living year-round **wherever** you call home, thanks to **creative,** doable ideas for every budget.

Creating outdoor living spaces for family and friends to enjoy is fast becoming a top priority for many homeowners and apartment dwellers alike. Perhaps our love for alfresco living began in the Garden of Eden, but wherever it started, our enthusiasm continues to grow. As a result, more people are improving, upgrading, and redesigning their properties, both as an investment in the future in terms of re-sale and as a way to increase their enjoyment of outdoor living right now.

## What Do You Have in Mind?

If you yearn for an airy haven, it doesn't matter whether you live in the country, the suburbs, or the city. Nor is the size of your property important, or how little money you have to spend. You can do so many things to improve your home and yard to increase their use and your pleasure in them. Sometimes it can be as simple as buying new furniture for the sun room or adding plants around the deck or balcony. Or you might consider undertaking an ambitious project, such as erecting a gazebo in the garden or putting in a pool off the back patio. Whatever your dreams, *What's in Style—Outdoor Living* is packed with enough inspiration, inventive professional advice, and glorious photographs to help you pull together and decorate a comfortable and attractive oasis that suits your fantasy.

Can you imagine yourself taking tea or an afternoon nap in your own English-style conservatory? Chapter One, "Light-Filled Rooms," presents a host of wonderful glass-enclosed garden rooms. Included are conservatories and sun rooms that are livable all year long, whatever the weather is like outside. If you're planning to add a garden room to your house or just want to include some garden style to an existing one, you'll find lots of great ideas and practical tips here. And if your decorating style is Victorian, you'll feel especially at home with many of the examples on display in this chapter.

Americans have long enjoyed porch living, and the romance continues. A porch can simply provide shelter from the rain, or it can function as a casual outdoor living room with a front-row seat to life in the neighborhood. In Chapter Two, "Porch Perfect," you'll find lots of decorating ideas—some traditional and some that are anything but traditional—for making all types of open and enclosed porches more welcoming and beautiful, and suitable to so many lifestyles.

Thinking about adding a patio or deck, or looking for ways to make the most of an existing one? These structures are great for connecting a house with its yard and gardens. Chapter Three, "Decks and Patios," covers it all. A stone- or brick-paved patio is a classic way to add an outdoor dining or entertainment area. In recent years, the deck has quickly become the favorite way to increase the living space of a house and freshen its style. Like the patio, deck design has improved over time. You'll enjoy seeing how to make either one appealing for today.

If you're an avid gardener, you already know the importance of having the space to devote to your favorite pursuit. Whether it's attached to the house or in a separate shed, a potting place can help transform your gardening chores into delightful pastimes. Chapter Four, "Potting Places," is filled with ideas for potting sheds and benches, as well as mudrooms.

Look to Chapter Five, "Structural Elements," for examples of handsome gazebos, pergolas, and arbors that give height, shade, and prestige to a site. These and many other "hard" landscaping elements, such as gates and trellises, also provide a focus, set a mood, and lend a crowning touch to any landscape.

There's just something mesmerizing about the presence of water, and it's been said that its addition can make any garden or yard feel magical. It could be a simple container pond or a large, in-ground pool, but Chapter Six, "Water Effects," presents the options available for including this feature in your outdoor life.

But water elements are only the beginning. When you're ready for the little touches, those that state your presence and personality, you'll want to study Chapter Seven, "Outdoor Adornment." There you'll find all types of creative ideas for adding unique embellishments and decorative accessories to your outdoor rooms. There are the usual and the unusual in this collection.

Once the hard work has been done, the pieces are in place, and the flourishes are set, you'll be more than ready to sit down and enjoy the fruits of your labor. Whether for solitary contemplation or the enjoyment of the camaraderie of friends, review Chapter Eight, "Successful Seating," and Chapter Nine, "Dining Out," for the latest ideas in seating and dining furniture, plus outdoor cooking. Whatever you need—chairs and benches, dining sets and picnic tables, love seats and side tables, brand new or antique—you'll find ideas and inspiration, as well as tips for equiping outdoor kitchens plus shopping advice.

## Are You Ready to Begin?

What are your favorite outdoor activities? Start a file folder of ideas. It will serve as inspiration for you and will provide direction for your designer or architect. Some of your ideas may seem unattainable now, but with a realistic schedule, you'll be amazed at what you can achieve. Good luck!

# 1

# light-filled rooms

As the Victorians did, you can **fashion** a lush, **exotic,** and faraway escape inside the privacy of your own **home.**

Do you dream of unwinding in a lush, light-filled space where it feels like springtime all year long? Whether it's a classic plant-filled conservatory, a versatile sun room, a wall of windows, or simply one spectacularly large window, an indoor room filled with natural light can lift your spirits by bringing sunshine and nature inside—particularly if there's a verdant view of the outside to enjoy. In fact, medical studies confirm what most of us have always sensed: the more natural light people live with, the better they usually feel, both physically and psychologically.

In addition, these light-filled airy spaces can act as pleasant transitions that link the house and garden. A garden room connecting a kitchen to a patio is a perfect breakfast area that provides a wonderful wake-up call, no matter what the season. A sun room overlooking the backyard makes an excellent sitting room or play area. Even a few well-situated, generous-size windows anywhere can blur the line between the interior and exterior of your house or the landscape beyond. Enter an urban apartment with a fabulous skyline view or a seaside cottage with windows overlooking the water, and you'll feel as if you've been transported. Conservatories, sun rooms, and windows can open our eyes and senses to the world outside. The Victorians recognized this and tried to re-create the feeling of faraway places with exotic plants and imported furnishings. This chapter offers ideas for accomplishing the same in your own home.

### What to Grow

**A** conservatory can extend the gardening season even in the coldest climates, as well as provide a place to cultivate delicate specimens that require a controlled environment. Orchids, camellias, citrus trees, jasmines, and gardenias thrive in the conservatory climate under the watchful gardener's care. Ferns, ivy, and palms are not as temperamental and add wonderful lushness. If you're not a seasoned gardener, they are excellent plants for you.

For the less ambitious gardener and culinary enthusiast alike, an indoor herb garden is an attractive and rewarding project. Grocery stores often sell potted herb plants in the produce section. Choose some of the seasonings you use frequently. Basil, rosemary, thyme, and cilantro are some easy-to-grow favorites. Re-pot them into a selection of terra-cotta containers, but keep the identification stake for watering and care instructions for each plant. Scented geraniums are also fun and easy to grow. There are many, and their fragrances vary.

## CONSERVATORIES

In eighteenth-century Europe, freestanding glass buildings, or orangeries, were constructed in the formal gardens of the grand manors to protect delicate exotic plants and fruit trees during the winter months. By Victorian times, particularly in England, the conservatory, by then usually attached to a dwelling, had become a status symbol. Heated by coal-burning furnaces, they required much attention in order to maintain the proper temperatures for keeping the tropical plants thriving.

In recent years, conservatories are enjoying a renewed popularity, thanks in part to technology. Insulated windows and efficient heating and cooling make the addition of a conservatory to your home an attractive and affordable option. Most companies that build conservatories provide design and engineering assistance, recommending the best location, style, and materials to suit the architecture and setting of your house. Styles can range from a simple lean-to room to an ornate Gothic edifice. Before undertaking a project, check zoning and permit requirements.

**Glass walls and ceilings,** above and opposite, afford a view of a garden outside or contain a garden within.

## SUN ROOMS

**W**hile a conservatory is usually an all-glass structure that may or may not be attached to a house, a sun room generally shares the roofline of the house and has one, two, or three walls of windows. Sun rooms original to many older homes are not insulated, so they can be too cold to use during the winter in all but the southern-most climates. Replacing old drafty windows with energy-efficient double- or triple-glazed units not only updates the overall look of the sun room but adds to its comfort level for almost year-round use anywhere. If yours, like many others, is located inconveniently on the side of a house with no access to the garden, consider installing French doors and a patio or deck adjacent to the new entry.

## BRING THE WORLD INSIDE

**W**hatever the view, the easiest and least expensive way to lighten up your home is to simply add windows. Looking for a way to add a garden room or sun room without literally adding on? Is there a small room in your house on an outside wall that serves no real purpose? Replace outside walls with glass, or install a

Today's **energy-efficient glazing methods** mean year-round use of rooms like those opposite, above, and below.

bank of windows. Other ways to transform a stuffy dark space into an airy and sunny room, nook, or corner include enlarging existing windows, substituting sliding-glass or French doors for solid-panel units, or adding a skylight or roof window. But consult an expert before planning changes that may affect structural elements in your home.

## Garden Room Planning

In general, think about how you want to use a sun space. For all uses but growing tropical plants, a conservatory with a southern exposure, which gets strong sunlight all day, will be hot, especially during the summer. You will need air conditioning and adjustable window coverings for when the temperature gets high if you plan to do much living in that room. Facing west, the room will be more moderate in temperature, except in the late afternoon, the sunniest time of day for this location. If the room faces east, the brightest, cheeriest hours are in the early morning. Avoid locating your conservatory on the north side of the house. It won't get any direct sunlight, and it may even be too cold to use most of the year.

When planning, also consider the architecture of your home, your budget, and the climate where you live.

**Architecture.** Research what is appropriate to the structure, especially if you live in a period home. If you are adding windows, try to match or complement existing ones. Most conservatory companies manufacture a variety of styles, from Victorian to contemporary, and provide on-site consultations.

**Budget.** As with any building project, costs can vary widely, depending on size, materials, and style. In general, the cost per square foot of constructing a conservatory is comparable to building a conventional framed room. Contact several companies for their catalogs, and study the

**Designer Tip**

"Marble- and stone-topped tables are perfect for use in these light-filled rooms. Warmed by the sun during the day, the tabletops catch leaf droppings and can stand up to the splatters of watering cans and plant sprayers."

—Lyn Peterson

range of prices and styles. Custom designs and options increase costs but may be worth the extra dollars.

**Climate.** A conservatory or sun room can extend your enjoyment of the outdoors in almost any climate. In areas where the heat becomes unbearable at certain times of year, an air-conditioned garden room that can be shaded with the use of protective blinds provides a pleasant escape from the sun. During wintry weather, a glassed-in room offers a cozy spot for observing the outdoor elements.

## Ideas for Creating Indoor Garden Room Style

The indoor garden room has the advantage of protection from the elements of nature, much like a covered porch or patio does. So your garden retreat is the perfect spot to combine your favorite elements: wicker or rattan furniture upholstered in lush floral fabrics, a sisal or hooked rug, and accessories with a garden theme. Plus, these furnishings are lightweight so you can easily move them back and forth between the house and garden— further blurring the boundaries of indoors and out.

Keep your eyes open for antique wicker or wire plant stands. They are getting more difficult to come by, although affordable reproductions of Victorian styles are widely available.

Don't forget to add interesting architectural elements to your indoor garden room. Bring a stone statue indoors. Use a section of substantial molding as a shelf. Plant trailing ivy in large metal or stone urns.

Bring "indoor" elements into the design. Display a collection of plates on a wall—traditional blue-and-white transferware or a vintage floral pattern, for example.

Include anything bird-related, such as beautiful birdcages (inhabited or not), a birdbath, framed prints of exotic birds, or a collection of birds' nests, and select plants suited to the amount of light the room receives.

The addition of a conservatory, such as the ones at left and opposite, will add space and light. Temperature and light controls may be necessary, however.

# a portfolio of stylish design

# porch
## perfect

People **everywhere** are rediscovering the relaxed **charm** and simple **pleasures** of a porch.

Whether open or screened-in, at the front, side, or back of a house, porches of all shapes and sizes seem to have a universal nostalgic appeal. Did everyone have a grandmother who lived in a house graced by a wide welcoming porch? Perhaps it's the memory of lazy summer days or warm carefree evenings spent rocking away on an old porch swing that makes the notion so attractive. Or it may be because in these hectic times we all share the fantasy of the come-and-set-a-spell state of mind that porches of all types evoke.

The concept of the porch dates back to Ancient Greece and Rome. In fact, the word "porch" is derived from the Latin *porticus,* meaning the columned entry to a temple or a public building. This could explain why so many of the grandest porches boast stately classical columns. However, the real precursor of the great American porch is more apt to be the veranda ubiquitous in the tropical islands that were once British colonies. Colonial builders in these hot-weather outposts added colonnaded one- or two-story porches to their buildings in order to provide shade from the strong sun and shelter from the torrential rainfalls.

Similarly, both for practical and aesthetic reasons, the porch became an important element in the architecture of the American South. Majestic Doric, Ionic, or Corinthian columns added elegance to Greek Revival homes, while the shade provided by overhangs offered relief from the sweltering sun. In both the South and the North, elegant porches graced Georgian- and Federal-style homes.

It wasn't until the later Victorian era, however, that the porch became a standard fixture across the country. Because many Victorian houses were built in resort areas, it only made sense that a love for outdoor living carried over at home resulting in a proliferation of porches. Besides, this was the perfect place for the ornate details the Victorians admired, and so the more gingerbread trim, the better.

Porches fell out of favor for several decades during the latter half of the twentieth century, due in part to spare modern architecture, which favors an economy of ornamentation, and the advent of air-conditioning. Today's return to traditional forms makes the porch an important architectural feature and popular as an additional living space.

## THE FRONT PORCH

From the humblest stoop to the grandest veranda, front porches welcome visitors and inspire passersby. Realtors use the term "curb value" to describe a house

Select porch furnishings that create the style you want—simple and sparse, left, eclectic and comfortable, below, ornate and delicate, opposite, or another favorite style.

## MORE HELPFUL IDEAS

### Adding an Enclosure

**D**o you want to add a screened-in or glass-enclosed porch to your home? Consider the following information and alternatives if a porch addition isn't possible.

• Think about adding screens or windows to an underused open porch. Even if you decide to have them custom-made, this is a relatively inexpensive way to maximize your living area.

• If your climate is so infested with annoying bugs that you aren't using your deck or patio as much as you thought you would, think about adding a roof or overhang to cover the area, and enclose the sides. You already have the flooring, you won't lose the view, and, guaranteed, you'll use the space more. Because this will affect the roofline of your house, consult with an architect or builder before embarking on this project.

• A screened-in gazebo is another option, especially for summer dining. If you already have a gazebo, nailing mesh screening and finishing it with lathe strips is a do-it-yourself weekend project. Ready-made and custom wood screen doors are available through catalogs, lumberyards, and many of the larger home-improvement centers.

that has drive-by appeal. Indeed, houses with front porches appear friendlier than those without this feature. A porch that is well designed complements the architecture of the house and serves as a visual and physical transitional area between indoors and outdoors.

The most basic front porch consists of a few steps leading to a small landing, typically protected by an overhang. Stoops are usually seen in urban settings, and in days gone by they provided a place for folks to congregate on summer nights. In colder climates, a stoop might be enclosed with glass to provide shelter from the elements and to act as an airlock.

The wide front porches of the South moved north during the Victorian era and became favorite features for suburban, resort, and country homes alike.

## THE ENCLOSED PORCH

**S**ince the development of mesh screening in the late 1800s, the screened-in porch has truly become a summer living room. With all of the advantages of its open counterpart, a screened-in porch offers a feeling of

**Enclosed porches overlooking spectacular vistas,** like the ones shown here, are treasures for you to enjoy at all times of the day, by yourself or with family and friends.

**Designer Tip**

"How to furnish a porch? It's not just with wicker or wrought iron. My porch houses my old kitchen table, a really good pine piece that has remained on the porch 24/7 for the last nine years and is no worse for the wear. The same can be said of an old Oriental rug I keep there, plus my Aunt Hilma's bamboo furniture, and a Welsh dresser laden with many pieces of my children's art."
—Lyn Peterson

oneness with nature along with the benefit of bug-free comfort. This makes it an ideal spot for visiting, reading, late-evening dining, and even sleeping during the warmer seasons. Usually located on the side or the back of a house, a screened-in porch is also more private than one that is open, and so it can be informal.

## Decorating Your Porch

The essence of porch living is relaxation, and the only basic furnishing requirement is a perfect place to sit, whether it's a classic rocker, a romantic swing, or a comfy wicker chair. Whatever else you add depends on your lifestyle. If your front porch is the place where packages and mail are delivered, you'll need a table or basket to receive them. If it becomes the summer family room, include tables and storage accommodations in your plan.

Porch décor should complement the style of the interior. Here are some typical looks for porches.

**Romantic.** Have you filled your cottage or country home

with faded floral fabrics, vintage wicker, and painted furniture? Well, bring some of those pretty things outside for the warm weather. Nothing is more alluring than a pair of chaise lounges with plush cushions and slinky throws. Accent with potted palms, fresh flowers, and candles. Keep a table nearby for soft drinks and tea cakes plus a cache of your favorite romance novels, and get ready to enjoy your summer idyll.

**Southern Veranda.** Inspired by the gardens of Charleston, this look combines traditional elements to evoke Southern hospitality. Pair elegant wrought-iron or rattan furniture with glazed chintz or tailored fabrics, such as toiles and stripes. Create a formal symmetrical look by flanking a doorway or the top of the stairs with tall topiaries or boxwoods in matching planters or urns.

**Rustic.** The key word is simplicity. Furnish a rustic porch with a painted wooden rocker, an old church bench, or a pair of Adirondack chairs. Add twig tables, a hammock, old lanterns, some baskets, and accent it with old farm implements to complement the simple charm.

**Victorian.** Pull out all the stops. Combine intricately woven wicker, ornate cast-iron furniture, and classical statuary. Tie together diverse elements with color. Accent interesting pieces, such as a tea cart, and hang ferns.

The country-style porch, above, is decorated with pillows, wicker, and macramé. The rustic porch, opposite above, has sturdy twig furniture. The bright red porch, opposite, is alive with color and flowering plants.

## Porch Maintenance

**B**ecause most porches are made of wood, they do require upkeep. From time to time and particularly if your porch is old, check it for dry rot and insect damage. Unfortunately, termites love porches almost as much as people do and, very often, older ones need extensive repairs. Once your porch is stable, finish it with paint or stain. This is one of the best ways you can preserve it. Your choice of colors will add to the ambiance and most paint companies now provide "period palettes" to help you make the best selection for your home.

# a portfolio of
# stylish design

# 3

# decks &
# patios

These **open-air rooms** are
relaxing and **enjoyable** under
the **sun**—or stars.

Like a porch, the well-designed deck or patio can add
functional space to a house while serving as a
transitional area between the interior of a home and
the exterior property. By providing a defined surface
for furniture and perhaps cooking equipment,
storage, or even a spa, a deck or patio becomes an outdoor room.
If you have the space, you may choose to combine a deck and a
patio to increase living areas, or one rather than both may suit
your needs. Size and shape are flexible for the most part, and you
can usually find a design that will be compatible with any size
property or even any type of terrain. As with all projects, the
dreaming comes first and then the planning.

For inspiration, look at the pictures in this chapter. Drive around
your neighborhood and make note of designs that you like and think
might be adaptable to your property. Take snapshots of your house
and yard. Sometimes it's easier to see what's needed when you're
looking at a photograph rather than the actual space and structure.
Observe the time of day that certain areas get sun or shade. Think
of the intended use for the outdoor living area. Will it be for cooking
and dining alfresco, to house a hot tub, to provide privacy, to enhance
a view, to serve as a sunning spot, or all of the above? Will it be a
family zone where the kids will play? Will you entertain there? How
often? For large or small groups? How much money can you afford
to spend on materials and labor?

The answers to those questions will affect the location, size, and
styling. Whether you do it yourself or work with a professional
architect, landscape architect, landscape designer, or building

contractor, it's crucial to consider all these issues so you'll be happy with the results for years to come.

A deck and a patio often complement each other, especially if multiple levels are involved. You might want to walk out of the house onto the deck and then continue down the steps onto a stone patio, which may lead to the pool and or a hot tub. Perhaps you want separate cooking and sitting areas. Here are the options.

## DECKS

The deck is a distinctly American invention. First popularized during the 1960s and '70s, decks were uninspiring at first in terms of design. But today's deck designs have evolved into handsome, dynamic additions to any style of house, enhancing and extending the homeowners' time for enjoying outdoor living.

How you want your deck to look and where you live will help you determine what materials to use. Decks are traditionally constructed of wood: western red cedar, redwood, pressure-treated southern pine, Alaska yellow cedar, and tropical hardwoods. You can paint or stain wood decking or allow it to weather naturally. But most wood needs some protection from mildew and ultraviolet solar radiation with a UV-inhibiting sealer and preservative.

If you're not committed to wood and you want your deck to be almost maintainence-free, consider using composite decking, which is a material made of natural fiber and recycled plastic. Some composite decking doesn't even require a stain or sealant. You can purchase a special detergent at a home center to keep it clean. Another material option, vinyl, won't warp or rot, and all the care it needs is a hosing down periodically.

Typically, a deck is located at the back of a house in

**Crisply painted deck floors and railings,** opposite, suit the style of many older homes. **The natural look of wood decking,** above right, is often best for more contemporary structures. **An outdoor umbrella,** right, provides adequate shade and style on a sunny deck.

order to provide the most privacy. If you have the space or if your lot is sloped, you might want to consider a multiple-level deck. This not only offers a more gradual transition from the entry level to the ground but also offers a way to create separate zones for different activities, such as barbecuing, dining, sunning, or soaking in a hot tub.

Railings are essential on raised decks, both for safety and for looks. So many attractive railing styles are available either as custom or standard elements that you can easily use railings to tie in the look of the deck to the architecture of your house.

A multilevel deck, above, accommodates a sloped site. Bold color, pattern, and material, as seen in the examples on the opposite page, illustrate how far you can take a patio's design to lift it from humdrum to spectacular.

## Decorating Your Deck

You can add personal style to any deck. If you're living with an existing one that looks dated and you don't have the budget to rebuild, there are ways to give the structure a face-lift minus much expense. Here are some ideas.

Refinishing. A natural or stained deck suits both rustic and contemporary architecture, while a painted deck blends in better with traditional homes. A painted deck, because it has a more porchlike appearance than a natural wood deck, usually complements an older home.

Architectural Details. Add romance with the detailing. Provide shade with a pergola or awning, or privacy with a trellis. Use sections of old fencing as a railing, or integrate other architectural fragments into the plan to add personality to your project.

Furnishings. No matter how much your deck is lacking in ambiance, you can transform it with furnishings.

**Designer Tip**

"Creeping thyme *(Thymus Serpyllum)* is excellent for planting between paving stones. It's sturdy, adds color, and releases a wonderful aroma when you walk on it. Its cultivar 'Annie Hall' has lovely purple pink flowers, 'Aureleus' has gold leaves, and 'Carol Ann' has gold variegated leaves and lilac-color flowers."

—*Miranda Smith*

Create a cozy cottage atmosphere on the beach or in the heart of the city or suburbs with a collection of country furnishings and accessories, for example.

**Plantings.** Clematis climbing up the trellis on your deck, pots of rosemary and colorful geraniums, and graphic spiky grasses by the pool are examples of how the plants and containers you choose for your outdoor spaces add to its ambiance. A deck provides the perfect locale for a lush container garden, especially in an urban area where garden space is lacking. Be sure to choose plants suitable for your climate and for the amount of light your deck receives.

## PATIOS

Whatever the size, style, or location of a home, the inclusion of a patio increases the appeal of the landscape. Although the paved areas in a yard are

MORE HELPFUL IDEAS

### Create a Courtyard

**C**reate a private walled-garden retreat with fences covered by climbing vines. Add height with trellises, and divide spaces with clipped boxwood hedges. Include an (almost) instant patio by digging away an area of sod and then covering it with a layer of sand and landscaping mesh to discourage weeds. Then cover it with pea gravel, and add a garden bench, statuary, and perhaps an antique or two. The result? European ambiance for even the most nondescript suburban yard.

part of a category that landscapers refer to as "hardscaping," you might prefer to think of them as the flooring of your garden rooms, providing a defined space for arranging furniture, a cooking area, and plantings. Plus, even the smallest patio can introduce an interesting shape, pattern, or texture to the grounds.

The forerunners of the modern patio were the formal terraces and courtyards connected to grand European estates. Today's homeowners want sophistication and style but prefer a casual setting for outdoor comfort. As you would with any interior room, consider your lifestyle and how your patio can enhance it. For example, if you'll be cooking outside, you'll need easy access to the kitchen; if you'll be using a hot tub or spa, you'll require a privacy screen if your lot isn't secluded.

Other practical matters will affect your plans and budget, too. For drainage purposes, even a flat site will need some grading to prepare it for a patio. Terraced into

**Designer Tip**

"During the cold winter months, I streamline my patio and deck, but I don't completely unfurnish them. I merely pare them down. After all, there will always be a warm day here or there, even in February. An old wooden park bench and curbside finds such as vintage wrought iron remain, as does a metal plant stand. In summer it's alive with color, and in wintertime it's part of a still life—empty clay pots and all. I even keep the dry pussywillow wreath in its place on the cedar shake shingles."

—*Lyn Peterson*

a steep slope, your patio will require a retaining wall. Before you proceed with paving or grading, however, refer to site plans for your property and follow local building codes. Your mason or contractor will know that the site should slope away from the house for drainage but might not be aware of the location of a septic system and any pipes or cables that need to remain accessible or be avoided when excavating.

## Paving Particulars

You have many choices as to what to use on the floor of your patio or garden room. For any of these paving

**A small corner,** opposite, has the appeal of a private courtyard. Tall plantings create a semi-enclosure. **A low wall,** above, allows a view of the water from a large formal terrace. Natural "pavers," right, are soft and pretty. Designs can be simple or complex.

## Art Underfoot

Make a simple geometric pattern with your flooring materials. Create a focal point in a courtyard or a small area of a patio by fashioning an intricate mosaic with tile, stone, or colored concrete. By combining elements and colors, a simple garden room floor becomes a wonderful work of art. Whether you commission a craftsman or do it yourself, you'll have a permanent art installation right in your own backyard.

solutions, the key to success is making sure that the surface you're paving is perfectly flat and prepared with a base of rough gravel and sand.

**Brick.** For a warm and classic look, nothing beats bricks. For paths and patios, use paving bricks. They are less likely than common bricks to crack and heave with the effects of winter weather and traffic.

**Flagstones.** Sandstone, bluestone, limestone, slate, and granite complement just about any architectural style.

**Pavers.** Concrete can be cast into molds to form individual pavers that mimic brick and cut stone. Strong, durable, and much less expensive than stone or brick, pavers are ideal for large areas.

**Tile.** Terra-cotta, quarry, and glazed tiles lend an Old World look to a garden and are a perfect paving solution for hot climates. If you don't live in a temperate area, use only those tiles that can withstand freezing temperatures and conditions, or limit your tiling to protected areas.

**Gravel.** Loose materials, such as river stones, pea gravel, and crushed stones, are easy to work with and relatively inexpensive. The final result is an attractive and versatile look—gravel looks just as appropriate in an English-style garden, a Southwest desert garden, or an Asian garden.

**Concrete.** While it might not seem like the most aesthetically pleasing solution, a cast-concrete patio has some distinct advantages and produces a very attractive patio floor. It's affordable, flat, quick to install, and can provide a base for other paving materials later on. The sleek look of concrete is perfect for contemporary settings, but it also works well with other styles.

**A pathway,** opposite, made of slate flagstones, leads the eye toward another part of the garden.

# a portfolio of
# stylish design

# potting places

**Grand or small in scale,
they're great for work, storage,
or even enjoying a cup of tea.**

Technically, a potting shed is a place where a gardener starts flats of seeds and repots plants. Every gardener knows, however, that it is also a nurturing, almost spiritual place where garden life begins. The perfect potting area is a special place for gardeners to perform their favorite tasks and to get their hands dirty. There should be a sink and a bench, a large bin for soil, hooks for hanging garden tools, and shelves and storage for containers and garden supplies. However, most gardeners are improvisers and can fashion a serviceable place for nurturing their hobby from whatever might be at hand—an unused table or bench placed in the corner of a deck or patio, for example, or a converted outhouse or shed not too far from the flower beds or the vegetable patch. A mudroom can also do double duty, especially because it has direct access to the outdoors and the flooring is typically an easy-to-clean surface, such as tile, stone, or brick, that's impervious to water.

While most potting sheds are fairly humble structures, their origins can be traced to the grand estates of nineteenth-century England, with their resident gardeners and requisite greenhouse. The seedlings were planted in the potting shed and later taken to the greenhouse to mature before being planted in the gardens. While today we have the option of purchasing flats of seedlings at garden centers, the self-sufficient farms and estates of yesteryear had to produce from seed enough food to feed the members of the staff and family, as well as all the flowers for making life enjoyable.

### Plotting a Potting Space

**W**hether you opt for a simple corner potting bench or a multipurpose shed or greenhouse, organization is key. You'll need a work surface—a counter or table that's a convenient height for standing while at work—plus storage accommodations for hand tools, long-handled tools, watering cans, extra lengths of hose, hose nozzles, flowerpots, bags of fertilizer and potting soil, gardening books, and notebooks. Plastic garbage cans (with lids) are good for soil and seeds. Most of these spaces are small, so use hooks and stacking bins which keep items neat and at hand's reach. High shelves free up floor space while holding least-used things.

At one time, outbuildings, from barns to lean-tos, were ubiquitous features of the American family farmstead. Suburban architects of the twentieth century, however, shied away from these utilitarian structures, often in favor of an attached garage. But as our love affair with gardening and the outdoor life grew, so did our need for additional storage. The response was the prefabricated

**Potting shed style** spans from old, weathered, and rustic, left, to new, built-to-match structures, above.

backyard shed. If there's no available outbuilding on your property just waiting to become your personal potting place, one of these readymade structures may be able to serve your needs.

No matter what your potting area is—a makeshift corner, a mudroom, a prefab shed, or a custom-built garden shed or greenhouse—if you spend a lot of time

**A plain and simple utility shed,** right, gains prominence and importance from its dramatic approach.

**Designer Tip**

"Does the size of your yard or budget preclude a separate structure? You could carve a corner out of the garage if there's a window nearby. But you need access to water. That's why a utility or laundry room can double as a potting place. Set a large shelf under the window for seedlings, and reserve a cabinet for storing supplies."
—*Marlene Wangenheim*

gardening, potting, or puttering around the yard, you'll need a workspace—or at least a bench—that's devoted solely to those activities, along with the necessary tools and supplies you should have at hand.

## POTTING SHEDS

In addition to functional attributes, there's something romantic about the notion of a potting or garden shed. Visually, it can be a focal point in the garden, framed by beautiful flowers and an abundance of vegetables. You can even entertain in there. Like other garden structures, such as pergolas, gazebos, and follies, the potting shed will add a strong vertical element to the overall design of your house, and it will introduce added architectural detail and old-fashioned charm to your outdoor area. Plus it can come in all sizes, shapes, and styles.

**Bright colors and interesting collectibles,** opposite, combine for a pleasant work environment inside a potting shed. **Proper siting** is more crucial to the success of a greenhouse, above, as it is for a potting shed, right.

While the word "shed" might suggest a run-down utility building, a garden shed can be grand or humble in appearance, either reflecting the architecture of other buildings on the property or setting its own tone. In the past, prefabricated sheds were utilitarian and affordable but not attractive. But over the years the choices in looks have improved dramatically. Whether offered by a home center, Web site, or a mail-order catalog, sheds of all types are available in an assortment of styles, sizes, colors, materials, and price ranges to fit a range of needs. For

Shelves, storage, and work surfaces are key elements of any successful potting area, whether it's located in the corner of a large mudroom, above, or garage, opposite.

a minimum investment, you can purchase a sturdy prefabricated wooden structure that complements the style of your house. Complete with windows, barn doors, and a wood floor, it can be a cost-effective way to acquire the potting shed you've always wanted.

Another way to go is to hire a landscape architect to design a custom structure that matches your house or is a rustic creation that can nestle into and combine with the landscape unobtrusively.

## Planning for a Potting Shed

The best time to plan for the inclusion of a potting shed or space is while designing the landscaping and garden areas. Even if you won't be building a shed right away, consider your overall needs, making sure the structure will be tall and large enough for you to stand, sit, and move around comfortably. Here are some other points to ask yourself while planning the shed.

• Will it actually be a place for starting and transplanting seedlings? If so, you will need light and a potting table or counter that is high enough so that you won't be bending uncomfortably in order to work.

• Will you store tools there? The walls will need to be tall enough to accommodate the longest rake or pitchfork handle. What about larger equipment, such as the lawn mower, garden tracker, or rototiller? Measure them to estimate how much square footage you'll need for all of them. You'll want a concrete floor, a wide doorway, and a ramp for easy entry, too.

• Do you also need a woodshed? Consider a combination wood, tool, and potting shed that has a concrete floor to keep rot, insects, and moisture away from stacked wood.

• You'll need access to running water, so unless you plan to include plumbing in your shed, find a location that's close to an outdoor faucet.

• How much strong sunlight will it get? Full sun could make the structure too hot during the summer months.

Cross-ventilation will help to keep your shed from becoming overheated, so consider placing two or more windows across from each other.

## POTTING BENCHES

Perhaps you don't have the space or resources to devote an entire building to indulging your love of gardening. A potting bench can be the ideal solution for you. Some hooks from which to hang tools and shelves for pots, soil, seed packets, and possibly a stool are all you need to add. Outside, locate the bench near a water source; indoors, place it close to a utility sink in the garage or basement.

You can purchase a potting bench from a garden supply catalog or Web site, custom-build one to your specifications, or draft an old table into use. In any case, make sure it stands at least higher than waist-height or elevate it to make it comfortable for you to work. If your bench isn't outside or near a window, you'll need artificial lighting aimed at an angle onto the surface to avoid glare. And if it's in a chilly spot, you might want to install a safe space heater nearby.

# a portfolio of stylish design

# structural
## elements

An outdoor **structure** can be **simple** or complex while bringing order and form to **outdoor spaces**.

Sometimes it's necessary to contain or "tame" nature. This is one reason why structure and focus are considered to be important features in landscape design. While free-form or wild gardens can be charming, the addition of even a single structural element can provide a focal point for a site, becoming the crowning touch in many cases. Depending on where you put it and what it is—a graceful gazebo, an imaginative tree house, or an evocative weathered gate—a garden structure can introduce symmetry, whimsy, or calm to an outdoor environment. Aesthetically, it can direct the eye of the viewer to travel from one place to another, such as in the case of a lush, vine-covered arbor that draws attention skyward while balancing other elements of varying heights. Besides visual stimuli, a structure can set a mood or help to define a style. Install a rose-covered arbor for Victorian or country-style "romance," or underscore Asian-influenced architecture with a pagoda-inspired pergola. Paint the finished structure for a refined look, or stain it to match a deck or to give a rustic feeling to your design. Add an element of fun or a touch of the unexpected by commandeering something like a vintage door or window for use as a privacy wall. Any type of structural element can help to define the physical space while introducing order to what might otherwise be a chaotic jumble.

In addition to adding ambiance to the landscape and organizing the space, structures can provide support for climbing plants and vines, shade for delicate plants, and welcome shelter for a garden's inhabitants. Throughout history and all over the globe, fascinating

structures from pavilions to pergolas have provided restful spots within the landscapes of parks, famous gardens, and private estates.

In Chinese gardens of long ago, the arrangement of rocks and man-made elements were more important than the plants and trees. Small temples graced even the humblest gardens. Ancient Roman gardens focused on sculptural features such as columns, statuary, and fountains. Protective walls surrounded medieval gardens. Renaissance edens were typically laid out geometrically and filled with structural elements from arbors to sculpted hedges and statuary.

The Victorians loved to include diverse items in their gardens. Everything from benches, bridges, and even buildings adorned the Victorian landscape. Well-heeled Victorians had a fondness for placing whimsical and ornate buildings in unexpected spots on their property. Sometimes miniature versions of their homes and other times reproductions of classic structures, these artful edifices, called summerhouses or follies, were evidence of the owner's wealth and exuberance for life.

**The gated arbor,** opposite, stands ready to welcome visitors to this garden. **An open pavilion,** left, offers a shady refuge for this sunny patio. **A unique gazebo,** below, has shoji-screened walls and doorway.

**Designer Tip**

"Create a natural rustic trellis that might even, if growing conditions are right, produce its own pretty blooms. Cut and place saplings in the ground as uprights. Then weave old grapevines with smaller saplings for the lattice."

—*Miranda Smith*

## ARCHES

**T**he simple charm of a garden arch can be sublime. Defining a welcoming entry into a garden as well as providing the framework for climbing plants, arches enjoyed wide popularity in Victorian times, and today they are a fixture in the gardens of casual cottage-style houses and sophisticated formal residences alike.

Carefully plan the placement of an archway. One that will lead into a fenced-in or walled garden should be planned to reinforce the feeling of entering a private space. Generally, if the archway will be near the house, it will make the best impression when it's lined up with the front or back door, even if the path between the two meanders.

Installing a garden archway is a weekend project. Catalogs and garden centers offer a wide array of styles in wood, metal, and low-maintenance vinyl. If you choose wood, moisture-resistant cedar or redwood is practical. For the most stable installation, set the posts in concrete. Be sure to follow local building codes as well.

## ARBORS

**A**n arbor is an open shelter covered with vines or branches. Whether it's constructed of bark-clad tree limbs in the rustic style or made of finished lumber and painted for a formal appearance, an arbor provides a perfect home for climbing roses, grapevines, or wisteria. Furnished with a small table and a few garden seats, the leaf-dappled effect formed by the light and shadows can enhance this Old World setting for alfresco dining.

If you indeed plan your arbor as an airy dining spot, consider using flagstone or pea gravel as "flooring." It will feel more like a garden room and will be less buggy than grass can be. When choosing the location, find a level area with easy access to the kitchen or grill.

**An arched doorway,** above left, and **a lengthy pergola,** left, direct attention to what's in the distance. **A tree house bedroom,** opposite, takes relaxation to lofty heights.

## PERGOLAS

A pergola tends to be more classical in appearance than an arbor and, indeed, dates back to ancient Greek and Roman times. Owing to these roots, its architecture is usually formal in style. With columns or posts as uprights and open beams serving as the "roof," a pergola can be freestanding or attached, and may provide support for climbing plants.

An attached pergola is a wonderful way to break up the open space of a deck or patio while also creating shelter from the sun's rays. Freestanding, a pergola can be a transitional structure connecting one part of a garden to another, or it can be a room on its own, providing a shady oasis within the landscape.

## GAZEBOS

Whether or not it's true that the word is derived from the phrase "gaze about," this is a lovely description of a gazebo. It truly is a wonderful place from which to gaze about the yard or garden. By definition, a gazebo is a freestanding structure with a roof and open sides. Egyptians built gazebos for meditation. In today's hectic world, a gazebo still serves as a restful retreat for the weary soul.

Sometimes square and other times hexagonal or octagonal, a gazebo can be formal or rustic in style, diminutive or grand in size. When planning your gazebo, as with other garden structures, consider the architecture and the overall landscape plan. For a gazebo situated near the house, for example, integrate the two structures by using the same roofing material. On the other hand, if your gazebo will be nestled in the woods, it can provide a magical woodland escape, so make it anything you like. When deciding on a location, remember the phrase "gaze about" as you envision the best place to relax in a comfortable seat while enjoying the view.

**Wood beams atop stone columns** create a handsome open-air room, below. **The Moroccan-inspired teardrop cupola,** opposite, lends an exotic ambiance to its setting.

## A Vine Romance

**M**ost vines, creepers, or climbing plants will ascend gracefully up your garden structure. However, some take longer to grow or require a stronger support than others. Consider the following information when choosing a climbing plant.

- For the romantic cottage look, nothing beats a climbing rose. Try the lovely 'New Dawn'. Its delicate pale pink blooms belie the plant's hardy exuberance. Climbing roses love rich, well-drained soil, and they need to be tied to whatever they are climbing on (arch, arbor, or trellis). Use sturdy string or wire.

- Wisteria requires patience and a strong support system. It usually doesn't bloom until the third year after planting and must grow on a porch or sturdy pergola—no flimsy trellis, please—but the rewards are really worth the wait. An established wisteria will produce masses of pendulous purple blossoms every spring for many seasons, and the vines become more beautiful each year.

- Climbing hydrangea, like wisteria, takes a couple of years to become established, but once it does, it makes a wonderful covering for brick and stone walls. Even when it has shed its pretty leaves, the vine forms interesting patterns on the wall.

- There are so many varieties of clematis that you might have them blooming all season. Most have showy, long-lasting flowers and make a bold statement when climbing up a front porch post or entryway arch.

## Rustic Style

Furniture and garden structures fashioned from unfinished logs, in vogue during the late 1800s, are back in fashion today. The natural look and relaxed feeling they evoke integrate beautifully with all but the most formal gardens. While you might think of the Rustic Style as an American genre, examples of twig furniture exist dating from ancient China as well as Renaissance Europe. An Appalachian legend claims that a weary traveler stopped to rest by a thicket of willows and made himself a chair to rest in, giving birth to the Rustic furniture movement. It was actually in the Adirondack region of New York, however, that American Rustic blossomed. Arbors, trellises, gazebos, and furniture made of unstripped twigs and branches complemented log cabins, grand and humble. Wealthy families, including the Vanderbilts, the Posts, and the J. P. Morgans, embraced the style for their country estates.

Twig furniture takes advantage of local resources, which appeals to the can-do approach of most craftspeople. Depending on availability in a particular area, woods as diverse as birch, magnolia, apple, and hickory are suited to rustic. Moisture-resistant woods such as white cedar stand up best to the elements.

# TRELLISWORK

In its simplest form, a trellis is a latticework panel used to support a plant or divide space in a garden. In seventeenth- and eighteenth-century European gardens, trelliswork, or treillage, abounded, adding structure and geometry to the landscape. Trellis makers constructed intricate garden architecture and the resident gardeners trained vines to grow in interesting patterns against the graphic latticework.

Today lattice panels made of wood or plastic are available in varying sizes at garden and home centers. Placed against a wall, a trellis adds texture and architectural detail in addition to providing support for plants and vines. Freestanding, a trellis can serve as privacy fencing, a windscreen, or a design element. It doesn't require a professional to design and install a freestanding trellis (there are even kits available), but you should set the supporting posts in concrete for long-lasting stability.

Functional and decorative, latticework can take on many styles and moods as displayed in the three different gardens pictured opposite, below, and right.

"Try a technique used by the royal gardeners at Versailles—espalier. They trained the fruit trees to grow flat against the walls, creating patterns. It's not difficult, especially if you go to a reputable nursery and purchase an apple or pear tree that has already been espaliered. Plant it against a flat surface that's in a sunny spot."

—Karin Strom

# a portfolio of
# stylish design

# water
## effects

A water feature **delights the senses** of sight and sound and creates **outdoor drama.**

To elevate your garden, deck, porch, or patio from mundane to magical, just add water. According to the design principles of Feng Shui, the ancient Chinese art of placement, the presence of water almost always brings forth harmony and prosperity. Whether or not you subscribe to this philosophy, there is no question that a water feature can add ambiance to your outdoor living environment. And while the sound of water is often soothing or relaxing, the sight of it can be dramatic.

Especially if you don't live near a body of water, consider the addition of a decorative or formal water element in your overall landscape plan. Just as the sound of waves on the beach often has a soothing effect on the soul, listening to the rhythm of water flowing from a fountain can quiet jangled nerves, while a pond may inspire reflection, and a birdbath may elicit a smile.

Your budget, the size of your property, and what effect you wish to create will help to determine your choices. Basically, almost any place can accommodate a water element. If you live in a city and have a small terrace garden, a self-contained fountain is a perfect antidote to traffic noise and provides an attractive focal point for your compact urban paradise. On the other hand, if your home is on a sprawling acre or two, a combination of more than one water feature and even a pool can help to define different areas and provide recreation as well as relaxation. A well-designed swimming pool adds a sense of luxury to a home; in combination with a hot tub or spa, it is the ultimate in outdoor luxury.

In ancient gardens, water was the central element in the design. The well or fountain served as a water source, gathering place, and focal point. Water features are so popular today that most garden centers have an entire section devoted to the do-it-yourself installation of simple ponds, fountains, and waterfalls.

Some retailers conduct workshops that can teach you how to install a water feature on your own. However, if you're lacking the time or skills required to do the work or if you're considering a more ambitious project, such as the installation of a hot tub or an in-ground pool, play it safe and hire a professional.

Stylewise, your approach to water elements—formal or informal—will depend on the overall design of your property. While not a rigid rule, if your home and grounds are classic in style, it's better to stick with a formal approach. But if they are casual and rustic in feeling, an informal look will be complementary to the overall design.

In general, formal design, in keeping with Renaissance ideals, is geometric and often symmetrical. Although many of the grandest gardens of the world, such as those in Versailles and the Taj Mahal, are formal, this approach is sometimes the most successful one to follow in the smallest places. For example, you could think about placing an octagonal pool in the exact center of a small garden. Or perhaps installing an ornate fountain on the wall of a city courtyard to transform an inconsequential small space into a dramatic oasis.

On the other hand, informal design strives for a less-staged effect and makes use of natural materials to achieve that goal. In that case, keep it simple. A pool, birdbath, or waterfall can fit into the environment as if it were always there, a look that is perfect for country and cottage settings.

## PONDS

Whether you have a small roof garden or a country estate, one of the easiest ways to introduce water into your outdoor design plans is with a pond. Aquatic plants add drama, and fish provide a source of endless fascination.

In the past, poured concrete was the only way to construct a backyard pond, and for a permanent formal decorative pool this is still the best method. But that job should be done only by a professional. With the variety of other materials available today, however, you can install a pond yourself with help from a good shovel and a flexible pond liner or preformed insert.

## FOUNTAINS & WATERFALLS

Moving water is relaxing to listen to and yet visually stimulating. You can create this in your outdoor room with a fountain or small waterfall. Both as a sculptural element and water source, a fountain can add elegance to any setting. Wall-hung

**According to Feng Shui principles,** round is the best shape for a pond. In the example above left, the spray of water adds energy to the design. **The wall fountain,** opposite, lends an Old World touch to this private courtyard.

"If a pond or small body of water already exists on your property, arrange your garden elements to take advantage of it. Build a bridge over it to connect it to other areas of the garden. If there's a dock already in place, make use of it for an instant midday picnic for one."

—*Karin Strom*

**MORE HELPFUL IDEAS**

## Do-It-Yourself Ponds

To avoid disturbing utility lines, contact your utility companies before doing any digging. Locate a freestanding container pond on your deck near an existing (GFCI) outlet. For an in-ground pond, have an electrician run a buried line and install a GFCI outlet near the pond so you can plug in a pump or fountain.

- For a basic freestanding pond, take a simple half-barrel and plastic barrel liner (available at garden centers) or a galvanized tub, and outfit it with a small submersible pump to aerate the water.

- For a natural-looking in-ground pond, use a flexible pond liner. To create a more realistic look for the edge of the pond, lay out a garden hose, moving it around until it forms a pleasant shape, and then dig the hole following the outline of the hose. Edge the finished pond with interesting rocks and plants.

and freestanding fountains are easy to hook up with the simple water-circulating pumps available in most garden centers. For a natural-looking waterfall that flows into a garden pond, use rocks gathered from your property and a circulating pump. Before you purchase a submersible pump, determine the size you need by calculating the gallon-per-minute flow of your pond. If that sounds complicated, don't worry. Garden centers that stock these items have this information. But be realistic. If it's necessary, hire a professional to do the job, especially when it comes time for the installation of any power lines and receptacles. In fact, depending upon your municipality's local codes and regulations, you may have to seek a qualified professional to help with some aspects of installing a water feature. It's also important to remember to lay electrical lines below the frost line in your area. Again, some localities require professional installation of branch circuits.

## SWIMMING POOLS

Many people regard having their own backyard swimming pool as a luxurious amenity. However, if you're wondering how a swimming pool will affect the resale value of your house, the answer depends on what part of the country you call home. If you are seriously considering making this investment, first ask yourself a few questions. For example, is your property big enough for a pool that will enhance rather than dominate the overall site? If your yard is small, a pool will be its major attraction. This could work to your advantage if you plan well and remember that you'll have to look at the pool all year long, not just during the hot summer

**A water garden and a bench** nestled in the corner of a patio, opposite, offer a great hideaway for relaxing. **A pond filled with water plants,** below, and surrounded by manicured plantings is a focal point in this formal garden.

## Instant Feng Shui

**P**ractitioners of the ancient Chinese art of Feng Shui believe that water is an excellent purveyor of Chi, or cosmic energy. This is especially true of moving water, which symbolizes cash flow and therefore encourages prosperity. When planning your landscape design and its water elements, consider the following information.

- Interesting rocks of varying shapes and textures contrast with the softness of the earth and movement of the water, balancing the yin and the yang in the garden.

- Swimming pools are less auspicious than natural-looking ponds that blend with the environment.

- Meandering paths reflect the natural movement of Chi. So plan gently curving paths rather than straight or angular ones.

- Less is more. It's far better to cultivate an interesting group of healthy and beautiful specimens that have a unifying theme, say all white-flowering plants or a variety of grasses, than to cultivate confusion with many different plants.

months. So, if you live in a cold climate, visualize how it will look in the winter when it's closed and covered over. Will it be visible from the house?

If you haven't worked with a landscape architect on your overall property design, this would be a good time to call one. It will add to the initial cost of the project, but it will be worthwhile in the long run, especially when you see how a landscape designer or architect can blend the pool into your property's natural terrain as well as with the style of your house. While swimming pool companies provide design and engineering expertise, they tend to be less concerned with a total concept than a landscape designer will be. The pool should be in an open and sunny spot, away from deciduous trees that will shed leaves into the water, for example. And it's practical to choose a location that is fairly level to minimize the need for costly ground work.

And what about the effect the pool will have on the

resale value of your house? As with most investments involving your home, consider how it will enhance your family's lifestyle, and then how it will affect the value of your property. If you see a pool as an ongoing benefit to the health and well-being of your family, it's probably a worthwhile investment. Also, if you live in a warm climate where the length of the swimming season is most of the year, you may find that a pool isn't just an amenity, it's a standard feature in today's market.

## HOT TUBS & SPAS

When used properly, hot tubs and spas can provide a great deal of relaxation and enjoyment. What's the difference between the two? A hot tub is a large barrel-like tub enclosed with wood. This amenity may or may not come with whirlpool jets, but it offers a deep soak of up to 4 feet. Many hot tubs come with an adjustable bench. A spa, which has an acrylic shell, can be freestanding, portable, or built into the ground or a deck. A spa is heated and typically jetted. One type, a swimming spa, is an in-ground unit that can range from 14 to 19 feet long, 7 to 9 feet wide, and 3 to 8 feet deep. A propulsion system creates a current. Deeper models are designed for aquatic exercises.

When determining the location of a hot tub or spa, consider the privacy factor, access to the house, water, and electrical power, and how to integrate it into your overall landscape. When possible, select the unit before building a deck so that the deck will fit around it.

# a portfolio of stylish design

# 7

# outdoor adornment

Use decorative **accessories** to bring **character** and personality to your space or to create **a theme.**

The careful selection and artful placement of a few well-chosen treasures personalizes and finishes off an outdoor area like nothing else. Whether it's as basic as a birdbath at the center of a humble herb garden or as grand as an arrangement of sculpture in a formal garden, the visitor's eye welcomes these landing spots to break up areas of foliage or lawn, wall, or walkway. After all, an inviting landscape design and outdoor living environment is more than plants and structures.

Archaeological evidence suggests that people have been adorning their outdoor spaces with decorative objects since the Stone Age, whether as an offering to a deity or a symbolic prayer, or purely for aesthetic reasons. For example, stylized animal carvings guarded doorways in ancient Egypt. Native Americans in the Pacific Northwest displayed totem poles to illustrate ancestral myths. The Greeks and Romans carved exquisite marble statues to beautify their environs, and for centuries various items, such as lanterns and Buddhas, have served as a counterpoint to Nature's beauty in Japanese gardens. Today you can find a vast array of antique, reproduction, and new objets d'art to accessorize and personalize your outdoor living rooms, patios, decks, and porches. Sometimes you may want to re-create the look of a specific style or historic garden, and the right accessories will go a long way in helping you achieve your goal. Or your aim may be simply to add some personality or humor to an outdoor space.

Just like the accessories you arrange inside your home to complement your decorating style, the things that adorn your exterior spaces reflect your unique personality. Whatever your garden style is—formal, traditional, rustic, refined, or a combination of them all—don't be afraid to go with your instincts when choosing and arranging objects of art or whimsy. Let your outdoor rooms reflect your style. For a pleasing arrangement, always defer to the principles of scale and proportion, balance, harmony, and line.

## GARDEN DECOR

There are no hard-and-fast rules about what to use to decorate the garden. It's all a matter of taste, and you can feel free to experiment with various items. Do you want to make a bold statement that you might not express inside your house? Nature itself is grand, so don't be timid when looking for objects in terms of scale. Bear in mind that something that looks huge in a small shop may be too small in proportion to your outdoor room.

**Designer Tip**

"Placement is everything with ornaments in a garden. Some elements are best sitting by themselves. Others are better when they are part of a cohesive whole, perhaps placed in the greenery at a corner or flanking a structure."
—*Judith Driscoll*

## Formal or Informal

Should your outdoor decoration be formal or informal in style? It's so hard to draw the line sometimes. Formal gardens are based on geometry, and as such they are orderly and organized. In a traditional or formal garden, just the placement of objects can create symmetry and add a sense of scale. Simply situating a pair of elegant planters on both sides of a front walkway adds formality to it. Although not always true, an informal garden tends to appear less planned and studied. Loose, asymmetrical arrangements of less-refined or homespun objects in a cottage or country garden underscores the casual mood.

## Color

Color is a dynamic tool that can have many different effects in the garden. It may serve as a unifying element, such as harmonizing a group of unmatched chairs all painted the same color, or it can make something the focal point—a whimsical purple pergola, for example. It can evoke moods or memories while also attracting a visitor's attention—a soothing robin's egg blue gate, an

---

**A ceramic elephant,** left, repeats the colors in the Moroccan tile wall of this patio. **An old bentwood chair minus its cane seat,** above, makes a unique plant stand.

energizing bright red bench, an evocative stucco wall stained Mediterranean blue. While white is perfect for many, it can sometimes appear too bright or blinding against other colors, particularly on a brilliant, sunny summer day. On the other hand, a color close in value to its surroundings could become lost visually. The lack of contrast results in a bland arrangement.

## Collections and Groupings

A group of like items displayed together makes more of an impact than one lone object. Consider a single finial on a tabletop compared with several shapely finials, each with its own interesting color of chipping paint. Likewise, a grouping of plants in various pots of all sizes is more interesting than a single planter.

# SHOPPING AROUND

These days it seems as if everyone is looking for antique garden ornaments. Classic statuary, ornate Victorian birdhouses, and graceful vintage cast-iron urns are getting harder to find. The hefty prices that desirable items can command make it somewhat daunting for ordinary mortals to compete with dealers and collectors. Fortunately, there are low-cost alternatives to garden decorating. You don't have to mortgage the family farm and buy the pricey marble angels that caught your eye at an estate auction.

## Something New

Garden centers, home centers, hardware stores, and merchandise wholesalers are wonderful sources for all sorts of new and affordable decorative garden objects. Mail-order catalogs and the Internet are places to look. In addition to terra-cotta pots, lightweight resin planters,

Reproductions in cast concrete, above left, weathered antiques, such as the shelves, birdhouses, and watering cans, left, and whimsical artifacts, like the bowsprit figurine, opposite, are all candidates for outdoor rooms.

and galvanized buckets and tubs, here are some other ideas of what to keep an eye out for while you're at it. **Reproduction Urns.** A shapely urn adds elegance to a front porch or garden vignette. Antique urns, usually Victorian, are expensive and extremely heavy. (They can also be costly to ship.) Fabulous reproductions, particularly those made of resin, are affordable, stylish, and lightweight.

**Statuary.** Antique statues are pricey and difficult to find. Commissioned sculpture also tends to be a major investment. Fortunately, wonderful reproductions are being made of cast concrete and reconstituted stone. Be aware, though, that cast concrete deteriorates after a few years of exposure to the elements. If you are a purist about what you place on your property, auctions can be a great

### Give It Another Chance

**B**ear in mind that even if an item has lost its luster, it can take on a new life in the great outdoors. And it often happens that something that looks tired when it's indoors can add a new and invigorating, or even eccentric, charm to a porch, patio, or garden room. A lone peeling wooden shutter, a section of fencing, an old metal headboard, a rusty bike—any of these items or others like them can find new life in the garden. While peeling paint adds to the charm of some of these things, a couple of new coats may rejuvenate or preserve others.

source. Auction houses occasionally conduct sales of garden antiques.

**Pedestals.** Pedestals are ideal vertical elements and lend stature to objects placed on them. It could be a section of fluted wood column, a marble sculpture base, or a fiberglass knockoff. Any object placed on a pedestal gains instant importance.

**Obelisks and *Tuteurs*.** Obelisks have been pointing toward the sky ever since Egyptians erected them in tribute to the sun god, and their classic shape continues to grace today's landscapes. Pillar-shaped frameworks, sometimes referred to as *tuteurs*, are both functional and sculptural, serving as a support for vines while training them to grow in the shape of the form.

**Sundials.** Although most cultures fashioned some way to mark the passing of time by using the sun, we have the ancient Egyptian worship of that luminary to thank for sundials. The graceful armillary sphere or the simpler horizontal style sundials are both gentle indicators of time.

**Antique cast-iron elements,** such as the ornate lawn roller at right and the elaborate planter opposite, weather well and look great in any outdoor room.

**Birdhouses.** It doesn't take long to fall for the charm of birdhouses. Not just for the birds, they are affordable, easily transportable, and available in a variety of sizes and styles. They can be made of wood, metal, or even plastic, and add whimsy to any place outdoors.

**Gazing Globes.** Staples in the Victorian garden, gazing globes are enjoying a rebirth in landscapes and gardens today. Originally hand-blown mercury glass, the new gazing globes are typically mirrored glass balls, displayed on wrought-iron or concrete pedestals. These colored spheres reflect whatever is around them, adding a magical perspective to the garden.

## Something Old

While yard sales and flea markets aren't what they used to be, they are still a great source of items that can add a fun touch to a garden vignette. Salvage yards and places that rescue great things from houses or buildings just before they are demolished can also be treasure troves for garden ornaments. If you're lucky enough to have a barn, garage, or an attic full of junk, take a look around with a fresh eye. Perhaps something that you overlooked the last time you poked around in there will jump out at you now. Here are some things to keep an eye out for.

**Plant Stands.** The Victorians' fondness for plant stands hasn't faded, and for good reason. What a perfect way to display a group of plants on a porch or an inside garden room. Wirework, wicker, and wooden plant stands all make frequent appearances at flea markets. Just be sure the one you buy is stable and can support plants that get heavy after you water them.

**Birdcages.** Those fabulous grand, ornate Victorian birdcages cost a fortune, but the smaller versions may be within your budget. If not, import stores often carry fun knockoffs. Some of them may not be sturdy or safe enough for birds, but their interesting shapes make them candidates for display. Remember not to leave lightweight items like these outdoors in exposed areas where a gust of wind could carry them away.

**Watering Cans and Farm and Garden Tools.** The beauty of these objects is twofold; not only do they have an innate gracefulness, they are functional to boot. Old watering cans have both nostalgic appeal and sculptural presence. Each one has its own distinct personality but will look its best when it's displayed as part of a grouping. Shovels, rakes, and hoes look great when mounted on a wall or simply leaning in a corner and, unless you've found a very old tool too delicate to use, can also come in handy when working in the garden.

**Architectural Fragments.** It doesn't take a green thumb to add interest to a garden by using salvaged pieces from old houses and buildings. A section of molding becomes a display shelf; an ancient gate doubles as a trellis; an ornate railing divides two areas of a garden. And don't feel as though your finds must serve a purpose other than to add a sense of history and charm to your surroundings.

**Weather Vanes and Lightning Rods.** Whether or not they are fulfilling their intended functions, weather vanes and lightning rods are popular items in a garden. On top of a barn or on the ground in the middle of a flower or herb garden, both antique and reproduction weather vanes and lightning rods can be folksy or sophisticated. Some are highly collectible as well. Look for ones that are handsomely aged with perhaps even a rusty finish.

**An aged hand pump,** left, is as decorative as it is practical in this garden. **Mixing the whimsical with the mundane,** opposite top, makes an interesting vignette amid the herb plants. **Even a simple bird feeder,** opposite bottom, creates a peaceful silhouette in a field of green.

## When You're Out Walking

**D**on't limit your shopping to commercial venues. Be sure to keep your eyes open when you walk on the beach, in the woods, or through the fields. The well-trained eye can spot potential garden ornaments just about anywhere. Holiday excursions are the perfect time for a scavenger hunt, and whatever you find becomes an instant souvenir of that trip as well as an interesting addition to your garden. Here are some suggestions.

- Look for abandoned birds' nests and feathers. But don't disturb the birds.
- Collect interesting rocks from your travels. They can become part of a unique rock garden.
- Take a walk on the beach at low tide. You might find driftwood and shells that weren't there during yesterday's walk.
- If you live in an old house, you'll often find vintage bottles and pottery shards when you're digging outside. In the days before door-to-door trash pickup, most homes had a backyard garbage dump, which can be a source of buried treasure today. Display what you find on a porch table as a conversation piece.

# a portfolio of
# stylish design

The kiss of the sun
for pardon
The song of the birds
for mirth
One is nearer God's heart
in a garden
Than anywhere else
on earth

# successful seating

Please yourself and **visitors** to your **open-air room** with the best seat in or out of the **house.**

Choosing seating for your outdoor living areas is as important as it is for the rooms inside your house, and many of the same criteria apply. In both cases, you'll want style, comfort, and quality. Plus, wherever your outdoor living room—on the deck, under the pergola, or in the garden beyond the gazebo—you'll need seating pieces that are not only inviting and attractive but sturdy enough to hold up to the elements. Besides sun, wind, and water, there are the assaults of winter to consider if you can't store furniture indoors for the season. Once you have the pieces you need, you'll want to arrange them in a way that is conducive to successful seating for dining, conversation, or simply relaxing. Whether you choose to surround a low table with a love seat and a pair of comfortable chairs and create an outdoor living room or simply set a charming bench beside your garden, the seating you choose will affect how you will live in that space.

The earliest garden bench was probably a rock or fallen tree stumbled upon by a weary wanderer. In some gardens the simplest seat may still be the best type for you. But today, because you have so many choices in terms of style, material, and color, it's worth considering all of your options before making any choices. Chairs and benches are available in such a variety of looks that it can be a little overwhelming. Decide what suits your lifestyle and your outdoor space. Budget may also determine your selection but shouldn't hamper it. There are lots of choices in all price ranges. The wisest thing you can do is comparison shop.

Picture yourself simply sitting on a rustic bench by the pond or relaxing in a lounge chair with a cool drink, watching the sun go down after a long day. Or imagine entertaining friends at an elegant soiree on the terrace. Whatever direction your fantasies take you will help determine your outdoor seating needs, as well.

## FIRST DECISIONS

In the past, choices were limited for outdoor furnishings. So how do you narrow down the many options you have today? To simplify your decisions, first think about where you want to place your seating. Many times this is the determining factor as to whether you'll need a single seat or a grouping. Then consider what style you want to set as well as how long you hope the furniture will last. Because furniture left outside must stand up to the elements, quality is important, and it's a good idea to choose the best you can afford. The information given here will help.

### Location

The closer your seating area is to the house, the more important they complement one another. Transitional

**Comfortable rockers on a porch,** above, are front-row seats to everyday neighborhood events. **A wooden bench,** opposite, is both an inviting garden seat as well as a dramatic background for a flowering vine.

**MORE HELPFUL IDEAS**

### Solitary or Social Seating?

**D**o you seek solitude or crave conversation? Is privacy paramount or is highlighting a view your goal? A single chair placed away from the fray inspires meditation, while a friendly grouping of seats invites fellowship.

Even the smallest yard can accommodate a corner for contemplation. Sometimes the simplest seating is the most appealing. A stone bench beside a backyard fishpond or a folding chair nestled in a glorious flower bed could prove to be the perfect solution.

Encourage conversation by arranging furniture in friendly groupings. Create an informal outdoor living room by placing a comfy love seat or couch and one or two cushioned armchairs around an all-weather coffee table. Things needn't match. In fact, an eclectic arrangement is often more inviting than a formal, matched grouping. And while outdoor furniture is always a great investment, an impromptu (albeit temporary) grouping is easy to make by refreshing discarded indoor furniture with several coats of paint. Not only does this give your old pieces a face-lift, it also helps protect them from deteriorating.

**Designer Tip**

"Too much of the same is too much! I prefer to avoid matched sets of outdoor furniture. Instead, I'll pair a cast-iron table with wooden chairs, for example. Another trick I use is to choose all the same chairs from one collection, but I buy them in several different finishes. Finally, when it comes time for chair cushions, I like to select fabrics that feel and look good together but don't necessarily match each other or that of the umbrella."

—Diane Boyer

spaces, such as decks and patios, link the inside with the outdoors and tend to be the areas where folks congregate, especially if intimate seating arrangements have been provided to encourage conversation. As you move farther from the house and out into the garden, seating areas are apt to be contemplative, and matching styles don't matter as much.

## CLASSIC SEATING

If your house is Victorian, you'll probably want wicker, wire, or ornate cast-iron furniture. Traditional wrought iron or crisply painted wood pieces are more suited to classical architecture styles such as Georgian and Federal, while funkier wood or twig seats complement the

**A twig chaise,** above, outfitted with cushion and pillows, suits the country style and rustic setting of this screened-in porch. **An open-slat wooden chair,** right, offers a comfortable perch for enjoying this garden.

farmhouse or cottage style. Sleek metal or streamlined resin styles have contemporary appeal, while teak and rattan pieces play up an exotic or Far East theme.

## Longevity

Furniture that is exposed to the outdoors has to be able to take a beating. Metal, wood that's been treated or painted (or naturally decay-resistant types such as teak, redwood, or cedar), and most synthetics will hold up fairly well with a minimum of care. Wrought iron and steel are strong, but rust can be a problem; aluminum and resin are affordable but lightweight. Delicate wicker and rattan and soft woods are better for a protected area such as a covered or enclosed porch.

**Seat Cushions.** Many chairs and benches are outfitted with cushions, the durability of which should also be considered. Coated fabrics are excellent because they dry

quickly and are sun-resistant. Today's versatile weather-resistant fabrics come by the yard, so you can make your own seat coverings and pillows, too. Canvas is another good choice, but it will fade with exposure to the sun. Remember that any fabric that is not weather- and mildew-resistant cannot be left outdoors. Consider collapsible seating pieces if you have a limited amount of space for storing furniture indoors during the winter.

## Style Specifics

It's true: you can buy those molded plastic chairs sold at the grocery store for less than $20 apiece. They're inexpensive, stackable, and lightweight. But with all the other great options out there, you'll probably want to have them on hand just for backup. To create a cohesive decorated look, you should concentrate on one basic furniture style. Here's a look at some of the most appealing types that are available.

**Adirondack Chairs.** Named after the Adirondack region of New York, these low-slung chairs look like they'd be uncomfortable when in fact they provide surprisingly pleasant seating. New or old Adirondack-style furniture is the quintessential nostalgic American look, and it's perfect for informal retreats like a deck. The characteristic wide arms provide a convenient landing spot for a soft drink or small snack.

**Twig Furniture.** Rustic and natural, twig furniture is crafted from unfinished wood, usually with the bark intact. Twig seating (chairs, benches, or chaise longues) can cozy up a country porch.

**Steamer Chairs.** Evoking images of sleek ocean-liner voyages, steamer chairs invite lounging poolside, on the patio, or on the lawn. Once made of teak, steamer chairs are now frequently constructed of other decay-resistant woods, such as white cedar.

**Rockers.** A fixture on front porches everywhere, rocking chairs invite relaxation. Just watch someone attempt to sit primly still in one of them. Rocking chairs once held a place of honor in households—it was the seat typically offered to visitors. Now you can make visitors feel welcome in this outdoor version of an American classic.

**Sprung Steel Chairs.** During the 1920s, soon after the end of World War I, many armament factories cleverly converted into manufacturers of metal furnishings. Those springy metal lawn chairs that evoke memories of backyard barbecues are the products of these efforts. Charming originals are still available at flea markets, peeling paint and all. Look in home centers and mail-order catalogs for brand-new reproductions that capture the same nostalgic appeal but wear better thanks to technology that has improved finishes.

**Bistro.** We have the French to thank for this clever, practical, and stylish design. Usually foldable, the bistro, or café, chair provides a perfect extra-seating solution. And it is easily tucked away when not in use. While antique examples have the charm of the original paint and detailing, inexpensive new versions abound.

## Benches

Just the thought of a garden bench has such a romantic appeal. Hidden in a private courtyard or overlooking a sweeping vista, a bench can evoke an image out of a nineteenth-century novel. It can also be a comfortable perch for time alone communing with nature, reading, or simply taking a break from chores to admire a pretty garden or listen to the birds sing. Charming benches, antique and new, are available in a wide array of styles and price ranges. Some of the classics are discussed here.

**Carved Stone.** Carved marble and granite benches had their place in ancient Roman gardens and Renaissance parks alike. While a stone bench may not be the most comfortable of seats, it integrates beautifully with the environment, holds up to the elements, and actually improves with age. These days most "stone" benches are

Pillows add comfort and color to a unique double-chair bench, above right. Folding bistro chairs, right, can be stored almost anywhere, inside or outside the house. A classic Adirondack chair, far right, with its wide arms and angled back, is known for comfort, charm, and durability.

actually cast concrete or reconstituted stone, but a stone bench, no matter what its material, is still a classic seat for all seasons, especially in a formal setting.

**The Lutyens Bench.** Sir Edwin Lutyens was the designer of perhaps the most widely recognized wooden garden bench. Painted or natural wood, its gracefully curved back adds elegance to any setting. Sir Lutyens also collaborated with English garden designer extraordinaire, Gertrude Jekyll.

**The "Park" Bench.** Usually made of wood slats supported by cast-iron arms and legs, affordable scaled-down park benches are available through on-line and mail-order catalogs and at garden and home centers.

# MATERIALS, QUALITY & COST

Outdoor furniture is available in such myriad styles, price ranges, and materials that choosing the right products may take time to narrow down options that are suitable for your needs. In general, if you want something that will last, go with the highest quality because it's usually worth the investment. Then, there is the issue of old versus new. Nothing matches the charm of antique garden furniture. Unfortunately, it has become so popular and so pricey that this is often no longer the most cost-effective solution.

If you love the vintage look but don't have the budget for it, consider purchasing one or two antique accent pieces to complement your new purchases. In general, new chairs tend to be more stable than antiques anyway. And besides, there are many attractive reproductions that offer the look without the high price tag. The information given here, describing the most popular materials used in outdoor furniture, should help you choose.

## Metal

For traditionalists, nothing beats the classic—wrought iron. Dining sets, lounge chairs, and even gliders go fast at yard and estate sales, often as the purchases of professional antique dealers who know quality when they see it. Even with their original paint, these pieces look terrific but usually have some superficial rust damage. A good going over with a wire brush and a couple of coats of enamel paint works wonders.

**Cast Iron and Aluminum.** Highly popular during the Victorian era, cast-iron furniture tends to be ornate. Settees and chairs in lovely naturalistic designs graced private gardens and parks. Today both antique and reproduction examples are fairly easy to find. The reproductions are apt to be made of cast or extruded aluminum that is lighter in weight and less expensive than cast iron. In addition, cast aluminum is rustproof, so it's a lower-maintenance product.

**Wirework.** Graceful wirework chairs and benches are better suited to porch and sun room use or at least should be used in areas protected from wind and water. The more substantial ones, however, can survive the elements better. For extra comfort, top them with cushions.

## Reed

Whether it's new or vintage, reed furniture—wicker, rattan, and bamboo—is comfortable, informal, and appealing, but vulnerable to the sun and water. There are so many fabulous-looking new examples around these days that, unless you're a purist, it's not usually worth the expense of repairing an antique. But if you must have antique or old pieces, keep your eyes open for Lloyd Loom furniture. It was so well made that even the oldest examples have usually remained stable. And if you've been lucky enough to have inherited a splendid piece or two, consider having it restored even if it's just for the sentimental value.

Because of its delicate nature, traditional wicker is perfect for use in protected areas. However, today there are two all-weather types of "wicker" that serve well in outdoor spaces: natural acrylic-coated wicker and a synthetic wicker look-alike, which is actually made from a resin woven material that's waterproof. You can also find handsome, practical look-alikes for rattan and bamboo that offer style without the headache.

## Plastic

Plastic is certainly the lowest-care material for outdoor furniture, but until recently the styling options were limited. Today both cast resin and PVC pipe are fashioned into handsome and practical styles. Easy to clean and long lasting, lightweight plastic is the way to go, especially when you have to move your yard furniture around or put it away when it's not in use. But remember: lightweight furniture can be easily damaged because it's susceptible to strong wind.

## Wood

The quality of wooden garden furniture varies even more than the styles available. Discount stores usually stock several good-looking pieces for around $100 each while some benches sold by high-end purveyors can cost up to $2,000. It's not so much the design that explains the great range in pricing as the types of wood and the quality of construction. Low-end chairs and benches are usually mass-produced of softwoods, such as pine, and often require assembly. Perfect as starter yard furniture, they'll last only a couple of years. Midrange pieces are generally made of redwood or cedar, preassembled, and hand finished. The most expensive, or "estate quality," furnishings are constructed of teak or tropical mahogany, assembled with mortise-and-tenon joinery, and often come with a lifetime guarantee. These will become heirlooms that you can pass along.

An openwork settee with a curved back, above, doubles as an interesting plant stand in this colorful container garden.

MORE HELPFUL IDEAS

### Contemporary Styling

Classic designs have charm but not always comfort. Most of the newer looks, however, have both in their favor. For poolside settings and to complement contemporary architecture, consider matte-finish bent steel shaped into handsome high-tech designs. Practical PVC forms lightweight lounges. All-weather acrylic fabrics stretched over cast- or extruded-aluminum frames make comfy sling chaises.

## Mesh and Strap Seats

For comfort and easy care in a lounge chair, consider mesh. Airy polyester mesh fabric is stretched over an aluminum or steel frame to form a sleek-looking and ultra-comfortable lounger. The same mesh fabric is used with padding for all-weather cushions and pillows.

Back in the 1950s brightly colored canvas strips were woven across wood frames to form classic folding backyard chairs. Later, woven synthetics fastened to lightweight aluminum frames were the classic 1960s style of lawn furniture. Today flexible extruded vinyl straps and aluminum or steel frames are fashioned into some of the coolest and most comfortable examples of contemporary styles.

# a portfolio of stylish design

# 9

# dining out

Set the **mood** for impromptu family
meals or an elegant **gathering**
with friends **alfresco** style.

A backyard barbecue, a late-afternoon tea party in the conservatory, or an intimate candlelit dinner on the patio, whatever you choose, dining outdoors is special. And now that you have your outdoor living room just as you dreamed it would be, or at least well on its way, it's time to start enjoying it after all the time you've spent planning, designing, building, and decorating.

Whether you're a lavish entertainer who loves to throw huge parties or someone who prefers more intimate gatherings, it's important to set up your outdoor room to suit your dining needs. Most folks are more comfortable locating their cooking and eating areas behind the house, removed from the scrutiny of passersby. But if all you have is a front yard or porch, there's a great view from the front balcony, or you live down a secluded country road, the front of the house might be the best location for your outdoor dining and entertaining after all. If you're an avid gardener, you might want to reserve the areas near the garden where you and your guests can appreciate the fruits of your labor while dining. Besides, pretty flowers and other plants are naturally decorative.

Private or public, alfresco dining has its own charms that will make anyone feel at ease, no matter where they are. Your lifestyle and personality will also help you determine what to do. Generally, dining and conversation spots that are close to the house tend to be more formal than eating and lounging areas by the pool. But if your house is really casual and your family totally laid-back, you might be inclined to choose a big picnic table no matter where it will be situated. It could also be that your home has a definite architectural style, and you want all the furnishings to reflect the character of the building.

## DINING FURNITURE

Finding just the perfect table and chairs can make or break your outside dining pleasure. There are many options ranging from the classic-but-casual picnic table and benches to a welcoming love seat and coffee table to matched dining sets for formal entertaining.

Before you go shopping—for new or used pieces—first measure the space you have in mind to get an idea of the size and shape of the table and chairs that will fit. Remember to allow enough room around the table for

Informal dining pieces, above, adorned with beautiful linens and comfortable pillows, set the stage for a spur-of-the-moment luncheon in this airy conservatory.

pulling out the chairs and for people to comfortably walk around with food. If you're considering storing the furniture, be sure that you have enough room nearby, perhaps in your garage or basement. Another option is to buy protective plastic covers that fit over the pieces.

### Size

Choose pieces that are in scale with the surroundings. It's usually not difficult to find furniture for a large outdoor area, and if there's room left over it gives you the opportunity to buy more pieces to suit your needs. For a small courtyard, patio, or balcony, consider small, perhaps folding, pieces that are easy to move out of the way when not in use. Bistro tables and chairs are perfect

for this purpose, too. They come in a range of fun colors and are easy to pick and put away, even if they don't fold down to a smaller size.

## Comfort

Comfort is essential. When shopping for an outdoor dining set, sit down and see if the table height is acceptable and the chairs are comfortable (and will continue to be through a long, leisurely dinner). Good back support is as important outdoors as it is inside the house. Seat cushions can add color and soften the look and feel of chairs and benches. If you plan to leave pillows and cushions outside, they should be covered in an all-weather fabric. Otherwise, keep a storage area in a convenient location.

## Durability

Even during the warm-weather months, furniture takes a beating. Heavy teak and redwood pieces, which can be difficult to move in and out of storage, mellow with exposure to the elements and will add some form to the landscape when they are not in use. But high-quality metal tables and chairs made from wrought iron or cast aluminum will hold up longer if you clean and scrape the surface and repaint them every few years or at least at the first signs of wear.

A white wicker chair and table, above, provide a welcome and comfortable resting spot for a gardener to enjoy a refreshing beverage between chores.

## Tabletop Surfaces

The surface of the tabletop takes the most wear and tear, and what it's made of is important to the overall life of the table. As is usually the case, certain materials are more long-lasting than others but are usually more costly as well. Here are some of the types of surfaces available today.

**Stone.** The toughest material for the top of an outside dining table (or countertop of an outdoor kitchen) is stone—marble, granite, and slate are favorites. The natural beauty of stone, polished or unpolished, integrates beautifully with the outdoors, but stone is heavy and serves best if it's intended for a permanent location.

**Wood.** If you love the look of wood, be sure to choose weather-resistant varieties like teak, redwood, and cedar. And be sure that the joints are secured with both glue and screws to ensure the longevity and stability of the piece. If you choose to paint your wooden table, use

**Designer Tip**

"A retractable awning mounted above an exterior door stands ready for creating an instant outdoor room complete with a roof. Outfitted with the appropriate furnishings and decorations, your "room" is ready for any party, come rain or shine."

—Barbara Ostrom

enamel paint or penetrating stain for the toughest finish. Or better yet, purchase a table that has been factory-painted. Paint applied during the manufacturing process contains a bonding agent that will make it last longer.

**Wicker.** It is preferable to keep natural wicker in a sheltered area, but all-weather resin wicker is tough enough to remain outside. Buy a piece of shatterproof glass cut to fit the top of your wicker table to provide a smooth surface for easier dining and cleaning.

**Metal and Glass.** Most metal tables have a metal-mesh or glass top, or both. Either material is easy to clean and maintain and provides a good dining surface. If it has a

There's a style of dining furniture to fit the mood of any setting: a city courtyard, opposite above; a secluded corner or an open space, above; a sunny contemporary patio, right; a Southwestern porch, opposite.

## Ideas for Entertaining

**W**hether an everyday family meal or a big party for 50, make it memorable and fun. With a world of options, it's easier than you think. Be imaginative with food and decoration. Although it is true that great hamburgers and hot dogs will taste good even if served on plain white paper plates, make the meal more fun by following a theme of some sort—color, occasion, or seasonal activity, for example. Be inventive with the basic elements as well as the extraneous touches, such as flowers and lighting. Here are some examples to get you started.

- For an all-American barbecue, set a picnic table with a patchwork quilt having red, white, and blue in it. Use similar colors for the napkins, and perhaps even bandanas. Include a star-studded centerpiece.
- Make a children-size dining set using an old door propped up on crates, and surround it with appropriate-size benches or chairs. Cover the table with brightly colored, easy-to-clean waxed or vinyl-covered fabric.
- If you're planning an elegant dinner party, move your dining room table outside and set it with your best linens, china, silver, and crystal. Add romantic lighting with candles in fabulous candelabras, and set a beautiful but small floral arrangement at each place setting.
- Design a centerpiece showcasing the flowers from your garden. Begin the arrangement with a base of purchased flowers, and fill in with some of your homegrown blooms. That way your flower beds will still be full of blossoms when the guests arrive.
- Base your party theme on the vegetables growing in your yard, and let them be the inspiration for the menu. When your zucchini plants are flowering, wow your family or guests by serving steamed squash blossoms. Or if the vegetables are starting to develop, lightly grill them with other young veggies—they have a much more delicate flavor than mature vegetables do.
- During berry season, host an elegant berry brunch. Serve mixed-berry crepes on your prettiest plates under the dappled shade of a favorite tree.

---

glass top, make sure it is shatterproof. Many of these tabletops are equipped to accommodate an umbrella; use a heavy and secure base for holding the umbrella.

## OVERHEAD PROTECTION

**D**on't let the sun or even rain put a damper on your outdoor dining. Awnings and umbrellas can provide protection from both. At night either adds a sense of intimacy by breaking up a large expanse of sky.

**A cushion-laden built-in bench,** opposite, becomes a great dining area when a table and chairs are set in front of it.
**Several mismatched pieces,** like the great-looking ones at right, can make wonderfully charming dining sets.

## Add the Extras

Simple or plain, it's the little conveniences and miscellaneous touches that push the dining experience to perfection. Here are some extra things to think about.

• You can never have too many serving trays when you entertain outside. For carrying food or drinks from the kitchen or the grill, trays are indispensable.

• A serving cart on wheels makes a perfect movable outdoor bar and provides an additional serving surface. Look for one at yard sales or buy one new.

• Chances are you won't have a sideboard, but a few small tables to hold excess items are great substitutes for one. They're also easier to position in the different places where you need them.

• For cooler weather or even a summer's evening with a bit of nip in the air, nothing beats an outdoor fireplace for comfort. You could build one into the house, but various types of stand-alone units are sold in home centers. To add a Southwest ambiance, consider a chiminea, a clay fireplace. Try burning some piñon pine, and you'll feel like you're in Santa Fe. Be sure to follow manufacturers' instructions when using these fireplaces. You might also have to store them during the winter.

• Pots of fragrant plants—lavender, scented geraniums, flowering tobacco, or jasmine—provide a sensual aroma. Flowers such as roses climbing up an arbor or trellis are beautiful, evoke a romantic feeling, and lend a delicate scent to the atmosphere as well.

---

Awnings are a more permanent solution and can be custom-made to fit large or small areas. Have them installed professionally.

Market umbrellas, available in a wide range of colors and sizes, have wooden spokes and a certain festive appeal. Aluminum-spoke umbrellas often offer the advantage of all-weather fabric. You can tilt many umbrellas to shift their position as the sun moves. With either style of umbrella, shop for the best quality you can afford so that you don't have to keep replacing it. And remember to secure it to its base, either provided in the table or by means of a separate, sturdy stand.

Another option for controlling sunlight is to install a pergola. It adds a roomlike quality to a deck or patio by providing an open-air ceiling complete with dappled sunlight or shade during the day. For more coverage, you may want to consider growing a vine over the structure. But remember, the fuller the vine, the more shade you will have. If you want to keep some allowance for sunlight, you'll have to periodically prune back the vine.

# OUTDOOR COOKING EQUIPMENT

Cooking outdoors has come a long way from simply roasting hot dogs and marshmallows over a campfire. Today's options fit everyone's needs, budget, and space limitations, from the smallest hibachi to a fully equipped outdoor gourmet kitchen. Follow any local restrictions concerning outdoor grills before installation.

## Hibachis

Living in the city does not have to stop you from enjoying outdoor living. If you have a balcony or a small courtyard, a simple hibachi and a bag of charcoal allows you to serve your guests a variety of delicious barbecued foods—burgers, small steaks, and grilled vegetables—just to name a few. Before using the hibachi, however,

---

**A successful outdoor kitchen,** opposite, uses components that are attractive yet durable and weather resistant.

**Designer Tip**

"Nothing adds romance and intrigue to an evening soiree like candlelight does. Include just a few candles for an intimate dinner. Use more for a larger gathering, placing one or more on each table. Scatter luminaries around the yard. As the beautiful evening dusk begins, light candles, a few at a time, so your eyes can adjust to the dimming light. Not only do the candles illuminate the night in a magical way but they can also keep bugs at bay."

—Karin Strom

check with your building supervisor and the local ordinances for any rules that may apply to its use.

## Kettle Grills

Now a classic, the kettle grill is also a good choice for balconies and small backyards. Fueled with charcoal and easy to move around, purists trust this old standby and many people even refuse to convert to the popular propane gas wagon grill. Kettle grills are available in a wide range of prices, sizes, and colors.

## Wagon Grills

Basic wagon grills use charcoal, but most are equipped with lava rocks and a gas canister. They range in price from a couple hundred dollars for a no-frills version to several thousand dollars for a high-end model. But even if you don't choose the super-deluxe version, be sure your grill is the best quality you can afford and has an electronic starter, temperature gauge, a work surface, and a snug-fitting lid.

## Outdoor Kitchens

Avid outdoor gourmets, especially those who live in year-round warm climates, sometimes select the ultimate outdoor kitchen complete with a refrigerator, built-in stove, sink, storage areas, and counters. Where necessary, have a professional install the appropriate gas and electric lines and outlets for all the equipment you intend to have in your outdoor kitchen.

# LIGHTING

If you want to safely enjoy your outdoor living area after the sun goes down, you'll need some lighting. An unlit stairway, path, or driveway can be frightening or dangerous at night. Solve this problem by situating a few tasteful light fixtures in strategic spots. Don't overdo it, though. You don't want to upset your neighbor's privacy or have your property lit up like a baseball stadium. Likewise during the day, the style of the light fixtures should add to the overall look of the house, not detract from it.

Consider your lighting needs while you develop your overall landscape plan. That way you'll be ready to have the electrical work done as your yard areas are being established. Have outdoor fixtures installed by a licensed electrician who will follow local building codes and has experience with outdoor wiring and knows how deep to bury the lines. Include several all-weather electrical receptacles protected by ground-fault circuit interrupters (GFCIs) in the deck, patio, or porch areas. This will allow you to plug in strings of lights for special occasions, as well as stereo equipment and other miscellaneous electrical items.

Colorful furniture, fabrics, and flowers, opposite and below, form cheerful, informal dining areas. Light fixtures, right, brighten outdoor rooms at night.

# a portfolio of stylish design

# resource guide

## Associations & Trade Groups

**APA-The Engineered Wood Association** *is a nonprofit trade association, the U.S. and Canadian members of which make a variety of engineered wood products. Primary functions include quality inspection and product promotion. Free brochures are available.*
P.O. Box 11700
Tacoma, WA 98411
Phone: 253-565-6600
www.apawood.org

**Brick Industry of America** *is a trade organization that offers information on the selection, use, and maintenance of brick. Its Web site is also a source of links to brick manufacturers and distributors.*
www.bia.org

**California Redwood Association** *offers extensive technical information about redwood, including grade distinctions, structural applications, and finishing characteristics. The association also has design and how-to help for consumers.*
405 Enfrente Dr., Suite 200
Novato, CA 94949
Phone: 888-225-7339
Fax: 415-382-8531
www.calredwood.org

**Interlocking Concrete Pavement Institute** *offers advice and information on interlocking concrete pavement materials.*
14441 Street NW, Suite 700
Washington, D.C. 20005
Phone: 202-712-9036
www.icpi.org

**Southern Pine Council** *is a nonprofit trade promotion group supported by manufacturers of Southern pine lumber. The Web site also offers construction details and building tips, complete project plans, and other helpful brochures and books.*

P.O. Box 641700
Kenner, LA 70064
Phone: 504-443-4464
www.southernpine.com

**Western Wood Products Association** *establishes standards and levels of quality for western lumber and related products in western softwood species. Technical information is available.*
522 SW 5th Ave., Suite 500
Portland, OR 97204
Phone: 503-224-3930
Fax: 503-224-3934
www.wwpa.org

## Decks & Fences

**Archadeck** *is a network of locally owned and operated remodeling offices specializing in custom decks, sun rooms, screened porches, gazebos, trellises, arbors, and other related outdoor products. The Web site also provides helpful information on hiring a contractor.*
2112 W. Laburnum Avenue, Suite 100
Richmond, Virginia 23227
Phone: 800-722-4668
www.archadeck.com

**DeckWeb** *is an Internet site that provides information on deck design, building, finishing, and furnishing. The site also offers directories of product manufacturers and deck designers. Through the Deck Forum Q&A message board, homeowners can post questions for professional deck builders.*
www.deckweb.com

**Hoover Fence Company** *is an on-line source of a wide variety of aluminum, chain-link, vinyl, and wooden fences, gates, and railings.*
P.O. Box 563
5531 McClintocksburg Rd.
Newton Falls, OH 44444
Phone: 330-358-2335
www.hooverfence.com

**Kroy Building Products** *manufactures vinyl decks, deck and porch railings, fences, and other vinyl products. Free literature, technical information, and specifications are available. Use its Web site to locate a dealer near you.*
P.O. Box 636
York, NE 68467
Phone: 800-933-5769
www.kroybp.com

**Timber Holdings Ltd.** *imports exotic outdoor hardwoods, including ipé and jarrah, under the brand name Iron Woods, which the company says offer unique resistance to decay and insects.*
2400 West Cornell
Milwaukee, WI 53209

Phone: 414-445-8989
www.ironwoods.com

**TimberTech Ltd.** *products combine recycled wood and polymers to form complete deck systems that include railings, fascia boards, and a variety of planking. Use its Web site to locate a dealer near you. The site also has links to a variety of other Web sites related to outdoor living.*
P.O. Box 182880
Columbus, OH 43218
Phone: 800-307-7780
www.timbertech.com

**U.S. Plastic Lumber** *produces recycled plastic and wood/plastic composite lumber and deck systems sold under the Carefree and SmartDeck brand names.*
2600 Roosevelt
Chicago, IL 60608
Phone: 312-491-2500
www.usplasticlumber.com

## Furnishings

**AGI Group, Inc.,** *has a varied selection of patio umbrellas and retractable awnings.*
1951 Porter Lake Dr., Suite E
Sarasota, FL 34240
Phone: 941-377-5336
Fax: 941-377-6516
www.shuttertime.com

**Campania International, Inc.,** *offers a large collection of planters, statuary, and garden ornaments in resin, pottery, and terra-cotta. The Web site displays a selection of pieces and will direct you to a dealer.*
www.campaniainternational.com

**Charleston Gardens** *(See Furniture.)*

**Frontgate** *(See Furniture.)*

# resource guide

**The Garden Cottage Company, Inc.**

*(See Furniture.)*

**Gardener's Supply Company** *is a source of plants, sculptures, and accessories such as a copper snow gauge and steel cone tea light holders for a snow-covered winter garden. You can order on-line or request a catalog.*
128 Intervale Rd.
Burlington, VT 05401
Phone: 888-833-1412
Fax: 800-551-6712
www.gardeners.com

**The Intimate Gardener** *(See Furniture.)*

**Kinsman Company, Inc.,** *offers an extensive selection of trellises, arches, obelisks, plant supports, and topiary frames, as well as birdhouses and feeders, plant stands, and terra-cotta planters.*
P.O. Box 428
Pipersville, PA 18947
Phone: 800-733-4146
www.kinsmangarden.com

**Pier 1 Imports** *is a nationwide retailer of indoor and outdoor furnishings and accessories.*
301 Commerce St., Suite 600
Worth, TX 76102
Phone: 800-245-4595
www.pier1.com

**Statue.com, Inc.,** *offers a large on-line assortment of statues, table bases, columns, plaques, fountains, urns, and planters in a variety of finishes.*
100 North Main St.
Edwardsville, IL 62025
Phone: 877-675-2634
Fax: 618-692-6775
www.statue.com

**Virginia Metalcrafters, Inc.,** *uses century-old methods in its manufacture of cast-metal items that include garden furnishings such as birdbaths, sundials, statues, and fountains. There is an on-line catalog and dealer locator. You can also request a printed catalog.*
1010 East Main St.
P.O. Box 1068
Waynesboro, VA 22980
www.vametal.com

**Wind & Weather** *offers a variety of decorative garden items, in addition to selling weather instruments. You can order on-line or request a printed catalog.*
1200 N. Main St.
Fort Bragg, CA 95437
Phone: 800-922-9463
Fax: 707-964-1278
www.windandweather.com

## Furniture

**BenchSmith** *produces mahogany or teak outdoor furniture and accessories. Browse its on-line catalog. Furniture includes instructions for easy assembly in usually less than 30 minutes.*
429 Easton Rd
Warrington, PA 18976
Phone: 800-482-3327
Fax: 800-518-2501
www.benchsmith.com

**Charleston Gardens** *offers a diverse array of wrought-iron and cast-aluminum garden furniture, wall and freestanding fountains, and miscellaneous garden features, such as arbors, edgings, statues, armillaries, and topiaries. You can shop on-line or request a printed catalog.*
61 Queen St.
Charleston, SC 29401
Phone: 800-469-0118
Fax: 800-532-5140
www.charlestongardens.com

**Frontgate** *provides extensive catalogs on outdoor*

*furniture, decor, and accessories, including grills and outdoor kitchen equipment, as well as a catalog for pools and spas. Browse products on-line or request a printed catalog.*
5566 West Chester Rd.
West Chester, OH 45069
Phone: 800-626-6488
Fax: 800-436-2105
www.frontgate.com

**The Garden Cottage Company, Inc.,** *offers an assortment of wood, resin, and metal furniture, garden accessories, and decorative elements, including sundials, weathervanes, birdbaths, and birdfeeders. Extensive product-care instructions are also available on the Web site.*
1211 Mt. Kemble Ave.
Route 202
Morristown, NJ 07960
Phone: 888-771-3455
Fax: 973-425-0054
www.gardencottage.com

**Hatteras Hammocks,** *a manufacturer of rope hammocks, also offers hammock stands, swings, and accessories. Browse its Web site for products and to locate a dealer near you.*
P.O. Box 1602
Greenville, NC 27835
Phone: 800-643-3522
Fax: 252-758-0375
www.hatham.com

**The Intimate Gardener** *is an on-line source of a large assortment of furniture, furnishings, and accessories for all types of outdoor rooms. Among other items, its product index includes: furniture (including wicker), grills and accessories, swings, gliders, electric and solar lighting, hammocks, statues, greenhouses, weathervanes, trellises, arbors, gazing globes, and hammocks.*
4215 North Sheridan Rd.
Chicago, IL 60613
Phone: 773-472-7066 (in IL);

800-240-2771 (outside IL)
Fax: 773-472-2043
www.theintimategardener.com

**Kingsley~Bate, Ltd.,** *manufactures teak outdoor furniture. An extensive line of benches, tables, dining sets, and lounging chairs, as well as a wide variety of lawn and garden accessories, can be viewed on the Web site. You can also search for a dealer close to your home, or request a printed catalog.*
5587-B Guinea Rd.
Fairfax, VA 22032
Phone: 703-978-7200
Fax: 703-978-7222
www.kingsleybate.com

**Ridge Rattan Furnishings** *manufactures a large selection of rattan and wicker furniture for outdoor and indoor use. The company offers a variety of fabric styles for the seat cushions and will mail samples to you upon request. It also will work with fabrics that you send.*
1267 Ridge Road East
Rochester, NY 14621
Phone: 716-544-2779
www.ridgerattan.com

**Telescope Casual Furniture, Inc.,** *makes a wide array of patio, deck, and garden furniture. Chairs, tables, and umbrellas are available in myriad of styles and fabrics. The Web site contains a product and retail guide.*
85 Church St.
Granville, NY 12832
Phone: 518-642-1100
www.telescopecasual.com

**Tidewater Workshop** *produces a variety of white cedar outdoor furnishings. The Web site has an on-line catalog and assembly and care instructions.*
P.O. Box 456
Egg Harbor City, NJ 08215
Phone: 800-666-8433
Fax: 609-965-8212
www.tidewaterworkshop.com

# resource guide

## Grills & Outdoor Kitchens

**Frontgate** *(See Furniture.)*

**The Intimate Gardener** *(See Furniture.)*

**Martin Industries, Inc.,** *produces a diverse line of Broilmaster grills and accessories. The Web site also features an outdoor kitchen system.*
301 East Tennessee St.
Florence, AL 35630
Phone: 256-767-0330
www.broilmaster.com

**Sub-Zero Freezer Co.** *manufactures a complete line of stock and custom refrigeration units. The Web site offers step-by-step design ideas as well as an extensive on-line product catalog. A list of distributors is also available.*
4717 Hammersley Rd.
Madison, WI 53711
Phone: 608-271-2233
www.subzero.com

**Weber-Stephen Products Co.** *provides a selection of gas and charcoal grills, plus a line of portables. The Web site will walk you through various lines as well as a product comparison. It also has recipes, information on grilling accessories, and a detailed buyer's guide.*
200 East Daniels Rd.
Palatine, IL 60067
Phone: 800-446-1071
Fax: 847-407-8900
www.weber.com

## Lighting & Speakers

**Intermatic, Inc.,** *offers an assortment of Malibu brand, easy-to-install low-voltage outdoor lighting fixtures and accessories for the yard, deck, walkway, and driveway. The Web site provides information for establishing an outdoor lighting plan.*
Intermatic Plaza
Spring Grove, IL 60081
www.intermatic.com

**The Intimate Gardener** *(See Furniture.)*

**Kichler,** *a manufacturer of decorative light fixtures, carries a variety of outdoor lighting fixtures for illuminating walkways, gardens, paths, and patios. Browse the company's on-line catalog or request a printed version.*
7711 East Pleasant Valley Rd.
P.O. Box 318010
Cleveland, OH 44131
www.kichler.com

**Rockustics, Inc.,** *manufactures a wide range of weather- and water-proof outdoor speakers set within rocks, terra-cotta planters, and other stonelike materials. Visit its Web site to browse its product line and to locate your nearest dealer.*
5080 Paris St.
Denver CO 80239
Phone: 800-875-1765
www.rockusticsinc.com

# Structures

**Archadeck** *(See Decks & Fences.)*

**Bella Vista Gazebos** *manufactures redwood gazebo kits.*
3358 Monier Circle, Suite 3
Rancho Cordova, CA 95742
Phone: 800-600-0299
www.qualitygazebos.com

**Environmental Concepts** *offers a variety of outdoor building plans, greenhouse kits, and greenhouse supplies and equipment. The Web site also provides information on planning and building a greenhouse.*
8 West Sunrise
Benton City, WA 99320
Phone: 888-326-8634
Fax: 419-793-4277
www.envirocept.com

**Florian Greenhouse, Inc.,** *services more than 200 dealers nationwide and produces designs for solariums and greenhouses. You can view a photo gallery of products on-line.*
Phone: 800-356-7426
www.floriangreenhouse.com

**Four Seasons Solar Products Corporation** *designs and manufactures conservatories, sun rooms, patio rooms, greenhouses, and deck enclosures. The Web site offers a photo gallery of products and a franchise locator.*
5005 Veterans Memorial Hwy.
Holbrook, NY 11741
Phone: 800-368-7732
Fax: 631-563-4010
www.four-seasons-sunrooms.com

**Summerwood Products, Inc.,** *provides a variety of precut kits for assembling a shed, cabana, summerhouse, or gazebo design. There are numerous configurations and options available with the kits.*
733 Progress Ave.
Toronto, ON
Canada M1H2W7
Phone: 800-663-5042
www.summerwood.com

**Sycamore Creek** *specializes in copper garden furnishings such as arbors and trellises. Many designs are available as do-it-yourself kits.*
P.O. Box 16
Ancram, NY 12502
Phone: 518-398-6393
www.sycamorecreek.com

# Water Gardens

**Beckett Corporation** *is a provider of water gardening pumps, supplies, and accessories. A visit to the Web site may help you design and install your own pond and configure a pump and filtering system to fit your needs.*
Phone: 888-232-5388
www.beckettpumps.com

**Waterford Gardens** *has a comprehensive guide for selecting aquatic plants and flowers for individual needs. The on-line catalog includes pond supplies and equipment. The Web site offers information on pond life and care.*
74 East Allendale Rd.
Saddle River, NJ 07458
Phone: 201-327-0721
Fax: 201-327-0684
www.waterfordgardens.com

**William Tricker, Inc.,** *specializes in water gardens and is a source of aquatic plants and pond supplies, pumps, accessories, statues, and underwater lights. The company also has a selection of tub gardens.*
7125 Tanglewood Dr.
Independence, OH 44131
Phone: 800-524-3492
Fax: 216-524-6688
www.tricker.com

# glossary

**Arbor:** An open garden structure that supports plants and serves as a transition between sections of a yard or as an architectural feature that complements the landscape.

**Arch:** An upright curved framework for supporting vines or climbing plants. Often used to mark an entry or transition area in the garden.

**Asymmetry:** The balance between objects of different sizes formed by their placement or grouping. When the scale is correct, an asymmetrical arrangement can be as pleasing as, but is less formal than, a symmetrical one.

**Balance:** In design, equilibrium of forms in a defined area. Relationships between objects in balance seem natural and comfortable to the eye, and balanced relationships can be symmetrical or asymmetrical.

**Building Codes:** Municipal rules regulating safe building practices and procedures. Generally the codes encompass structural, electrical, plumbing, and mechanical remodeling and new construction. Inspection may be required to ensure conformity to local codes.

**Chiminea:** An outdoor fireplace made from clay and dating from seventeenth-century Mexico.

**Conservatory:** A glass building used to display and protect exotic plants and trees, especially during the winter months. Most often attached to a house, its glass walls and roof are held together with spokes of wood, vinyl, or metal.

**Courtyard:** An enclosed, usually small, patio.

**Dry-Laid Walk:** A masonry path installed without mortar.

**Espalier:** The training of a plant to grow flat against wires, often against a wall or framework. A plant so trained is called an espalier.

**Exposure:** The intensity, duration, and variation in sun, wind, and temperature that characterize any particular site.

**Feng Shui:** The ancient Chinese practice of placing and arranging elements for the purpose of promoting harmony and balance.

**Focal Point:** The dominant element in a space, such as a garden or landscape element, that draws the attention of viewers.

**Folly:** A small, whimsical building, often resembling the main house of a property. Popular during Victorian times, the building sometimes was a reproduction of a classic structure. Also known as a summerhouse.

**Footing:** A poured-concrete foundation for a heavy structure such as a deck, gazebo, or shed.

**Formal:** A style of landscaping that features mainly symmetrical forms and placements.

**Frost Line:** The maximum depth to which frost freezes the ground. Local building departments can provide information on the frost line depth in an area.

**Garden Room:** A defined outdoor space usually bordered by hedges, plantings, structural elements, or walls, creating a sense of privacy or seclusion.

**Gazebo:** A framed structure with a peaked roof that is usually hexagonal or octagonal. A gazebo offers roofed protection from the rain and sun and stands alone or is attached to another structure, such as a deck.

**Gazing Globe:** A colored mirror-glass sphere, displayed on a pedestal, to reflect whatever is around it in the garden. Staples in Victorian gardens, they used to be made of hand-blown mercury glass. Some of today's gazing globes are made of stainless steel.

**Greenhouse:** A glass- or plastic-enclosed building used for horticultural purposes. A greenhouse is usually a freestanding building set near a working garden and is less formal than a conservatory.

**Hardscaping:** Elements of a landscape other than plants, such as walks, walls, and trellises, that are made of wood, stone, or other materials.

**Hibachi:** A portable charcoal brazier with a grill that is used for outdoor cooking.

**Hot Tub:** A heated barrel-like, water-filled enclosure with or without whirlpool jets, and most often featuring a simple, adjustable bench. It offers a deep soak, and its acrylic liner usually is set into a wood exterior.

**Informal:** A style of landscaping that features mainly asymmetrical forms and casual placements.

**In-ground Spa:** This type of spa can be set into the ground or a deck, and its acrylic shell comes with a variety of seating arrangements and in a number of colors. The shell is supported by poured concrete, gunite, shotcrete, or fiberglass.

**Liner:** A plastic or rubber sheet used to create a watertight foundation for a pond or pool.

**Mudroom:** A transitional space between the inside and outside of a house for the purpose of shedding dirty footwear and outerwear before entering the home.

**Patio:** A paved surface most often located off the dining, living, or family room.

**Pergola:** A tunnel-like walkway or seating area with columns or posts to support an open "roof" of beams or latticework. It can be freestanding or attached to a building; it usually serves as a support for climbing vines.

**Portable Spa:** A self-contained, aboveground tublike unit with jets that runs on a standard 120-volt electrical circuit. It typically has an acrylic spa shell and a wooden surround for support.

**Potting Shed:** A small building used for storage, starting plants, and performing other gardening tasks.

**Pressure-Treated Lumber:** Wood that has had preservatives forced into it under pressure to prevent rot and repel insects.

**Proportion:** The relationship of parts or objects to one another based on their size.

**Retaining Wall:** A wall built to hold back and maintain a terraced area.

**Scale:** The size of an object as it relates to the dimensions of the surrounding objects and space.

**Spa:** A tublike structure featuring whirlpool jets that circulate hot water. Spas are available as in-ground or freestanding units.

**Sun Room:** A room along the side of a house sharing the roofline of the house and having one, two, or three walls of windows.

**Symmetry:** The identical arrangement of parts, objects, or forms on both sides of an imagined or real centerline. Symmetrical arrangements appear formal.

**Trellis:** A latticework garden structure used as a light screen, as a support for climbing plants and vines, or to divide space in a garden.

**Tuteur:** A handsome, pillar-shaped framework on which vines are trained to grow. It is both functional and decorative.

# index

# index

# index

# photo credits

page 1: John Glover **page 2:** Jessie Walker **page 5:** John Glover **page 6:** Jerry Harpur; designer: Gunilla Pickard **page 7:** *top left* Brad Simmons; designer: Morse; *top right* Positive Images; *top middle* Jerry Harpur; *bottom middle* Brad Simmons; *bottom* John Glover **page 9:** John Glover; designer: Andrea Parsons **page 10:** Tim Street-Porter/ Beate Works **page 11:** John Glover **pages 12-13:** Tria Giovan **page 14:** *top* Phillip Clayton-Thompson; *box* courtesy Rockustics Inc. **page 15:** John Glover **page 16:** Mark Lohman **page 17:** *top* John Glover; designer: Andrea Parsons; *bottom* Jerry Harpur; designer: Maggie Gundry **page 18:** Jerry Harpur; designer: Park Farm **page 19:** John Glover; designer: Andrea Parsons **page 20:** *top left* Tria Giovan; *top right* Jerry Harpur; designer: Maggie Gundry; *middle right* Meyer/LeScanff; Garden Picture Library, *bottom right:* John Glover; designer: Andrea Parsons; *bottom left* John Miller; Garden Picture Library **page 21:** *top left* Michael S. Thompson; *top right* Mark Lohman; *middle right* Nancy Hill; courtesy of Bob Vilas American; *bottom right* Tria Giovan; *bottom left* Nancy Hill; designer: Diane Burgoyne Interiors **page 22:** Jessie Walker **page 24:** *top* Brian Vanden Brink; designer: Jack Silvero, Architect *bottom* Brad Simmons **page 25:** Brad Simmons **page 26:** Brian Vanden Brink **page 27:** *all* Jesse Walker **page 28:** Brad Simmons **page 29:** *top* Brad Simmons; *bottom* Brad Simmons; *box* Brian Nieves/CH **page 30:** *top left* Brad Simmons; *top right* Mark Lohman; *bottom right* Jesse Walker; *bottom left* Grey Crawford/ Beate Works **page 31:** *top left* Jessie Walker; *top right* Brian Vanden Brink; designer: Stephen Blatt, Architect; *bottom right* Brad Simmons; *bottom left* Nancy Hill; designer: Stephanie Stokes, Inc.; *middle left* Jessie Walker **pages 32-33:** Brian Vanden Brink; Hearst Special Publications; designer: Centerbrook Architects **page 34:** Jessie Walker **page 35:** *top* Brad Simmons; architect: Greg Staley; landscaper: Barry Wehrman; stylist: Cindy Martin; *bottom* Jessie Walker **page 36:** *top left* John Glover **page 37:** *top* Tim Street-Porter/ Beate Works; *bottom* Phillip H. Ennis Photography **page 38:** *bottom* Grey Crawford/ Beate Works; *box* courtesy of Wind & Weather **page 38:** *top* Brian Vanden Brink; designer: Ron Forest Fence; *bottom* Grey Crawford/ Beate Works **page 39:** *bottom:* Brad Simmons; designer: Lila Weinburg, IIDA **page 40:** Brad Simmons; designer: Lila Weinburg, IIDA **page 41:** *all* John Glover; *bottom right and middle* designer: Karen Maskell; *bottom left* designer: Alan Gardner **page 42:** *top* Charles Mann; *bottom right* Charles Mann; *bottom left* Jessie Walker **page 43:** *top left* Mark Lohman; *top right* Nancy Hill; *bottom right* Walter Chandoha; *bottom left* Brad Simmons; *middle left* Brian Vanden Brink; designer: Ron Forest Fence **pages 44-45:** Jessie Walker **page 46:** *bottom* Brad Simmons; *box* courtesy of Charleston Gardens **pages 46-47:** *top* Alan & Linda Detrick Photography; designer: Pat & Scott Warren **page 46:** *bottom* John Glover; designer: Alan Titchmarsh **page 48:** Brad Simmons **page 49:** *top* John Glover; *bottom* Brad Simmons; designer: F. Fogg **page 50:** Brian Vanden Brink; designer: Scholz & Barclay Architects **page 51:** John Glover **page 52:** *top left* John Glover; *top right* Brian Vanden Brink; designer: Scholz & Barclay Architects; *bottom* Brian Vanden Brink; designer: Carol Wilson Architects **page 53:** *top left* Jerry Howard/ Positive Images; *top right* Brad Simmons; *middle right* Mark Lohman; *bottom right* Mark Lohman; *bottom left* John Glover; designer: Susy Smith **pages 54-55:** Jerry Harpur; designer: Richard Hartlage Graeme Hardie **page 56:** Jerry Harpur; designer: A. Pfieffer **page 57:** *top left* John Glover; designer: Robin Templar Williams; *bottom* Jerry Pavia **page 58:** *top* Ken Druse; *bottom* Brian Vanden Brink; designer: Payette Associate Architects **page 59:** Jerry Harpur; designer: Larry and Stephanie Feeny **page 60:** Edifice Photo/ Gillian Darley **page 61:** *top* Jerry Harpur; designer: Richard Timewell; *box* courtesy of California Redwood Association **page 62:** *top* Michael S. Thompson;

*box* courtesy of Moffett's Crafts, Country Collectibles, & More **page 63:** *top* Jessie Walker; *bottom* John Glover **page 64:** *top left* Charles Mann; *top right* Phillip Clayton-Thompson; *middle right* Crandall & Crandall; *bottom right* Walter Chandoha; *bottom left* Brian Vanden Brink; designer: Bullock & Company Log Home Builders **page 65:** *top left* Edifice Photo/ Phillipa Lewis; *top right* courtesy of Summerwood Products; *bottom right* John Glover; *bottom left* Brad Simmons; designer: Allison & Associates; stylist: Cindy Martin **pages 66-67:** Jerry Harpur; designer: Zea Berry **page 68:** John Glover; designer: Pamela Woods **page 69:** John Glover; designer: The Chelsea Gardener **page 70:** *top right* Brad Simmons; architect: Greg Staley; landscaper: Barry Wehrman; stylist: Cindy Martin; *bottom left* Charles Mann; *box* courtesy of Wind & Weather **page 71:** Edifice Photo/ Gillian Darley **page 72:** Edifice Photo/ Gillian Darley; *box* courtesy of Charleston Gardens **page 73:** Brad Simmons; architect: Greg Staley; landscaper: Barry Wehrman; stylist: Cindy Martin **page 74:** *upper left* Charles Mann; *upper right* Jessie Walker; *bottom right* John Glover; designer: Pershore College of Horticulture; *bottom left* Brad Simmons; designer: Marilyn Coombe Stewart **page 75:** *top* Alan and Linda Detrick; designer: Zea Berry; *bottom right* Jerry Pavia; *bottom left* Jerry Harpur; designer: The Chelsea Gardener **pages 76-77:** Tria Giovan **pages 78-79:** *bottom* Jerry Harpur; designer: Majorca **page 79:** *top* Patricia J. Bruno/ Positive Images **page 80:** *top* Jerry Harpur; design: Peter Causer Brighton; *bottom* Phillip Clayton-Thompson **page 81:** Jerry Harpur; designer: Tim Vaughan **page 82:** *bottom* Edifice Photo/ Philippa Lewis; architect: Victorian Roller; *box* courtesy of the Netherlands Flower Bulb Information Society **page 83:** Jerry Harpur; designer: Malcolm Hiller **page 84:** Edifice Photography/ Philippa Lewis **page 85:** *top* Alan and Linda Detrick; *bottom* Brad Simmons; *box* courtesy of Gardener's Supply Company **page 86:** *top left* Edifice Photo/ Sarah Jackson; *top right* Nancy Hill; courtesy of House Beautiful; *bottom* Jerry Harpur; designer: John Wheatman **page 87:** *top left* Phillip Clayton-Thompson; *top right* Brad Simmons; *middle right;* Charles Mann; *bottom right* Tria Giovan; *bottom left* Phillip Clayton Thompson **pages 88-89:** Positive Images/ Gay Bumgarner **page 90:** *top left* Jessie Walker; *box* courtesy of Telescope Casual **page 91:** Jerry Harpur; designer: Gunilla Pickard **page 92:** *top* Brad Simmons **pages 92-93:** *bottom* Positive Images/ Gay Bumgarner **page 94:** *top* John Glover; designer: Fiona Lawrenson; *bottom* Tria Giovan **page 95:** *bottom* Michael S. Thompson **page 97:** *top* Tim Street-Porter/ Beate Works; *box* courtesy of Kingley~Bates **page 98:** *top left* Jessie Walker; *top right* Tria Giovan; *bottom right* Charles Mann; *bottom left* Phillip H. Ennis Photography **page 99:** *top left* John Glover; design: Dan Pearson; *top right* Jessie Walker; *bottom right* Jerry Harpur; design: Oliver Allen; *bottom left* Tim Street-Porter/ Beate Works **pages 100-101:** Jerry Harpur; designer: R. David Adams **page 102:** Tria Giovan **page 103:** Brad Simmons **page 104:** *top* John Glover; designer: Jonathan Baillie; *bottom* Mark Lohman **page 105:** *top left* Jerry Harpur; designer: Michael Balston; *top right* Mark Lohman; *bottom right* Grey Crawford/ Beate Works **page 106:** Stephen Harby/ Tim Street-Porter/ Beate Works **page 107:** *top* Nancy Hill; courtesy of House Beautiful; *bottom* Jessie Walker **page 108:** *top* Nancy Hill; *bottom* Roger Turk **page 109:** Tim Street-Porter/ Beate Works **page 110:** Jerry Harpur; designer: R. David Adams **page 111:** *top* Michael S. Thompson; *bottom* Jerry Harpur; designer: Keeyla Meadows **page 112:** *top left* Jessie Walker; *top right* Jerry Harpur; designer: Mary Effron; *bottom right* John Glover; designer: Alan Titchmarsh; *bottom left* Jerry Harpur; designer: Katie Kend **page 113:** *top* Juliette Wade/ Garden Picture Library; *middle right* Stephen Harby/ Tim Street-Porter/ Beate Works; *bottom right* Jeremy Samuelson; *bottom left* Brad Simmons **page 125:** Derek Fell

# Have a home improvement, decorating, or gardening project? Look for these and other fine Creative Homeowner books at your local home center or bookstore.

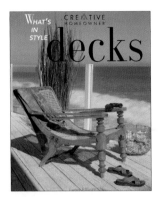

The latest in deck design and deck products. More than 200 color photos and illustrations.
128 pp.; 8½"×10⅞"
BOOK #: 277183

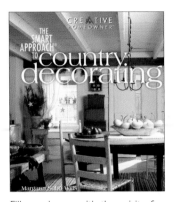

Fill your home with the spirit of country: fabrics, finishes, and furniture. More than 200 photos.
176 pp.; 9"×10"
BOOK #: 279685

Transform a dated kitchen into the spectacular heart of the home. Over 150 color photos.
176 pp.; 9"×10"
BOOK #: 279935

How to work with space, color, pattern, and texture. Over 300 photos.
256 pp.; 9"×10"
BOOK #: 279667

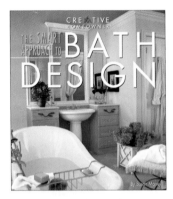

All you need to know about designing a bathroom. Over 150 color photos.
176 pp.; 9"×10"
BOOK #: 287225

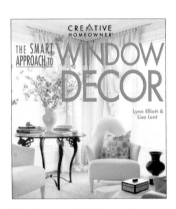

Get the practical information you need to choose window treatments. Over 100 illustrations & 125 photos. 176 pp.; 9"×10"
BOOK #: 279431

Turn an ordinary room into a masterpiece with decorative faux finishes. Over 40 techniques & 300 photos. 272 pp.; 9"×10"
BOOK #: 279550

Interior designer Lyn Peterson's easy-to-live-with decorating ideas. Over 350 photos.
304 pp.; 9"×10"
BOOK #: 279382

Impressive guide to garden design and plant selection. More than 600 color photos.
320 pp.; 9"×10"
BOOK #: 274615

Lavishly illustrated with portraits of over 100 flowering plants; more than 500 photos.
208 pp.; 9"×10"
BOOK #: 274032

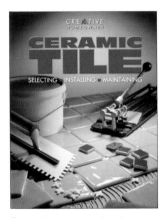

Everything you need to know about setting ceramic tile. Over 450 photos and illustrations.
160 pp.; 8½"×10⅞"
Book #: 277524

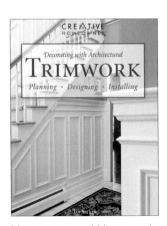

How to create a richly textured home. More than 450 color photos and illustrations.
208 pp.; 8½"×10⅞"
BOOK #: 277495